SOCIAL SCIENCE SEMINAR SERIES

Raymond H. Muessig and Vincent R. Rogers, Editors

THE VOLUMES AND THE AUTHORS

The Study of Anthropology, Pertti J. Pelto

Political Science: An Informal Overview, Francis J. Sorauf

Geography: Its Scope and Spirit, Jan O. M. Broek

Sociology: The Study of Man in Society, Caroline B. Rose

The Nature and the Study of History, Henry Steele Commager

Economics and Its Significance, Richard S. Martin and
   Reuben G. Miller

THE CONSULTANTS FOR THE SERIES

Anthropology, George D. Spindler

Political Science, Charles S. Hyneman

Geography, Jan O. M. Broek

Sociology, Arnold M. Rose

History, Henry Steele Commager

Economics, Kenneth E. Boulding

SOCIOLOGY
THE STUDY OF MAN IN SOCIETY

Caroline B. Rose
Department of Sociology
University of Minnesota

Arnold M. Rose, *Consultant*
Department of Sociology
University of Minnesota

*With a Concluding Chapter Suggesting Methods
for Elementary and Secondary Teachers
by* **Raymond H. Muessig** *and* **Vincent R. Rogers**

CHARLES E. MERRILL BOOKS, INC.   COLUMBUS, OHIO

Library of Congress Catalog Card Number: 65–21164

3 4 5 6 7 8 9 10 11 12 13 14 15-76 75 74 73 72 71 70 69 68 67

PRNTED IN THE UNITED STATES OF AMERICA

Social Science Seminar Series

Edited by Raymond H. Muessig
and Vincent R. Rogers

The Social Science Seminar Series presents scholarly viewpoints on and information about history, geography, political science, economics, sociology, and anthropology. This social science material is complemented by creative and practical methods, tailored to each of the individual fields, for elementary and secondary teachers.

One assumption built into these six volumes is that the social studies program in our schools should reflect more faithfully and sensitively the social sciences from which it is derived. It is imperative, then, that social scientists contribute their suggestions regarding over-all content selection problems in the social studies.

A second premise inherent in the Social Science Seminar Series is that professional educators are responsible for translating appropriate social science substance into meaningful and enriching learning experiences for children and youth. In their contacts with the editors of this Series, the contributing social scientists repeatedly made the point that they could discuss their disciplines only as they saw them and not in the light of what should be done with them in the schools. It is the professional educator—thoroughly prepared and broadly experienced in thinking about and coping with educational theories, problems, and practices—who must weld a framework that will support understandings, skills, attitudes, and appreciations drawn from or tied to the social science disciplines. It is the educator, too, who must decide what can and should be taught at various grade levels and how this subject matter might be conveyed, buttressed, and assessed by a myriad of suitable methods, materials, resources, and evaluative processes.

There is a critical need in both pre-service and in-service teacher education programs for up-to-date, clear, stimulating material concerned with recent developments in the social sciences. Teachers should see these disciplines as spheres of continuing scientific study and inquiry, rather than as hardened, static, sterile bodies of accumulated fact. Further, they must obtain a more sophisticated grasp of the goals, scope, importance, and interpretation of these fields as well as some understanding of the concerns faced by those working in a given field. The Social Science Seminar Series encourages and assists teachers at all instructional levels to critically examine their purposes in and approaches to the teaching of specific areas of content fundamentally related to the disciplines treated.

With this perspective in mind, the editors of the Series suggested that each of the contributing social scientists ask himself what his field really does contain that professional educators should consider teaching to youngsters. Each author was asked to describe the nature of his field; to trace briefly its history, development, and maturation; and to look at its unique methods of working as well as those procedures shared with other social sciences and related fields. Most importantly, each specialist was requested to select out of mountains of data a series of fundamental, compelling ideas that have emerged from his field.

In each volume of the Social Science Seminar Series, the editors have written a final chapter to accompany the discussions and analyses of the social scientists. The editors have *not* attempted to build an overarching theory of social studies education; rather, they have concentrated upon specific, functional classroom methods. The concluding chapters in this Series, therefore, do not present a total program, a master theory, a blanket plan of attack, or an endorsement of the proposals of any single group endeavoring to improve social studies instruction. The generalizations the editors have chosen to illustrate should not be viewed as the basis for a course or sequence of offerings. The ideas they have introduced transcend particular topics, units, themes, or curricula. Careful exposure to them can support many learnings. The editors have not dealt at this time with *why, how much, where,* and *when* questions regarding the place of individual social sciences in the social studies family today or tomorrow. As they see it, each social science can be taught by itself in breadth or depth, woven into existing scope and sequence patterns for development or supplementary purposes, or assigned manifold roles in some yet-to-be-developed curriculum design.

Space limitations have not permitted the exhaustive treatment of a single idea, problem, or approach drawn from each of the social sciences represented. Instead, the editors have suggested a number of procedures that could be used or adapted for use in a variety of elementary and secondary school situations. It is not intended that the techniques offered in the Series be employed in a one-a-day, isolated, disjointed, decontextualized fashion. A superficial flitting from one major insight to another would have little meaning for students and would possess limited retention or transfer value. It is not expected that pupils will comprehend abstract generalizations in a definitive sense after an occasional lesson or two. The editors believe that global ideas should be approached, discovered, introduced, developed, and confirmed in different ways and contexts and at increased levels of complexity throughout the school years. They have taken into account the fact that it takes time, patience, and systematic organization to build durable learning.

The Social Science Seminar Series, then, should function as a point of embarkation—inspiring and challenging readers to keep abreast of developments in the social sciences and in social studies education.

Preface

There are many definitions of the term "discipline" as applied to various academic fields of study. If applied to the area of sociology, one of the most popular explanations would read that "Sociology is what people who call themselves 'sociologists' study." On the surface, this homespun definition might appear to be satisfactory. Yet it really is not very helpful. Even a cursory exposure to sociological writings, research projects, and course offerings should impress one with the futility of trying to fit all sociologists into any single pigeonhole. Many sociologists find themselves spending a good deal of their time developing abstract theories, concepts, models, and so forth. Theories must be tested as well, and when sociologists move out of this rarefied, highly theoretical realm, they find that they must test their hypotheses on *people*. Other sociologists are not engaged in research but rather attempt to deal directly with concrete situations in schools, hospitals, factories, prisons, urban ghettos, remote farm areas, and other settings.

We believe that sociology has a crucial role to play in helping children and youth understand the complex, social world in which they live. We further believe that many of sociology's insights, ideas, concepts, and generalizations *can* be understood to varying degrees by many learners. This book is the culmination of the extended, cooperative efforts of a sociologist and two social studies educators. The first five chapters, on the discipline itself, were written by Caroline B. Rose of the University of Minnesota. Mrs. Rose traces sociology's origins and development; she also discusses representative sociological schools of thought, theories, issues, and methods of attack and observations. The last chapter, on classroom methodology, was written by Raymond H. Muessig of the College of Education at The Ohio State University and Vincent R. Rogers of the College of Education at the University of Minnesota. Focusing on a group of basic generalizations drawn from Mrs. Rose's preceding five chapters, Professors Muessig and Rogers propose and illustrate numerous approaches that teachers might employ to help elementary and secondary school students gain some understanding of these sociological observations. Arnold M. Rose of the Department of Sociology at the University of Minnesota served as academic consultant for this volume.

The Editors

vii

Table
of
Contents

The Nature of Sociology   chapter one

SOCIOLOGY IS THE STUDY OF GROUP LIFE

Men everywhere live in groups. This is fortunate for sociologists because the consequences of group living are the subject matter of sociology. Their interest in groups is what distinguishes sociologists from other scientists. Among other things, sociologists want to know why groups like the family, the tribe, or the nation persist over time even during war or revolution. Why does a soldier fight and face death when he might hide or run away? Why does a man marry and take on responsibilities for a family when he might just as easily satisfy his sexual impulses outside of marriage? What effects does group living have on the behavior of group members? Do people who live in isolated, preliterate tribes behave differently from those who live in New York or a Parisian suburb? Are the attitudes of a slum dweller different from those of an upper-class businessman and, if so, why?

Sociologists are equally interested in why groups change or fall apart. For example, they want to know why some marriages end in divorce. They are interested in why there is more divorce in some countries than there is in others and why the rates of divorce increase or decrease over time. They want to know if people behave differently after they move from the country to the city or from the city to the suburbs.

Finally, sociologists study the relationships among group members and among groups. What are the relationships between husband and wife and between parents and children in the United States today? Are these relationships like those in the early American family or like those in families in other countries? What

1

causes conflict between Negroes and whites in the South? Do labor, industry, and government in the United States relate to each other in the same way as do similar groups in Australia or the Soviet Union? Why do some groups in the society have more material goods and more prestige than do others?

SOCIOLOGY IS ONE OF A GROUP OF SOCIAL SCIENCES

Sociology is a science, and sociologists, like all other scientists, try to explain the phenomena within their field and to test their explanations. Anthropology, economics, political science, history, and geography are the other social sciences, and with each of them sociology has many common interests.

Anthropology and sociology are specialized branches of the same science. Anthropologists have usually studied preliterate or nonindustrialized societies, and sociologists have concentrated on the study of complex, modern, industrial societies. Each science has invented research techniques suited to study the kinds of groups in which it is interested. Both sociology and anthropology examine group or social behavior. Or, as it may be alternately stated, both sciences study man's culture. The basic theory in both sciences is the same.

Certain kinds of human behavior are studied by both sociologists and economists. For example, institutional economists and sociologists are interested in how and why labor unions develop the way they do and in their relationship to other groups in the society. Both are concerned with the types of personality that develop and predominate in a capitalist society, where competition is an important value.

Similarly, sociologists and political scientists are often interested in the same phenomena. The study of public opinion is of equal interest to them. So is voting behavior or the structure of political parties.

For a description of any social act that does not occur within immediate experience, sociologists are dependent upon historians to tell them what occurred. When historians are wrong, sociological theory will be wrong. In 1935 W. E. B. Du Bois, a famous historian, published a book called *Black Reconstruction*. It became evident that if the facts in *Black Reconstruction* were correct (they were heavily documented and are generally accepted by both historians and sociologists today), then the facts previously presented about the history of the Negro in the United States could not be true. Among other things, Du Bois stated that the Negroes elected to

Congress from the South and to Southern state legislatures during the Reconstruction Period after the Civil War were an educated group and that the legislation they enacted was sober, intelligent, and progressive. Negro legislators were not field hands, right out of the cotton fields, ordering gold spittoons for the state houses, as historians had reported. Sociologists then had to discard their theory that a large part of the antagonism between whites and Negroes in the South was the result of lack of education and irresponsible legislation on the part of Negro representatives during Reconstruction.

The relationship between sociology and geography is complex. American geographers have not traditionally been interested in examining the effects of the physical environment on the inter-relationships among men, although European geographers have. What changes in social life occur when the city is extended outward by the invention of mass transportation? In what kinds of city neighborhoods is there juvenile delinquency? When a neighborhood begins to change from residential to commercial, what happens to the families living there? To examine these and similar questions neglected by geographers, a special science, human ecology, arose within sociology. Today, ecology is a separate science, taught in departments of sociology, geography, and, sometimes, economics. Ecologists know a great deal about how a city changes and grows, and it is unfortunate that they are not asked for practical advice more often. They could point out to city planners, for example, that a device to raise land values in the blighted areas in our core cities would improve the character of the areas in a short time and would save the money and red tape involved in laboriously trying to reconstruct these areas. Ecologists also have a great deal of information about how transit routes develop and their relationships to the distribution of people. If this knowledge were used in laying out freeway routes, city administrators would be more successful in reducing urban sprawl and stopping the flight of people and money from the cities to the suburbs.

Psychology is the study of individual behavior and is not considered a social science. There is, however, a close relationship between one of the subdivisions of psychology—social psychology—and one of the basic fields of sociology, also called social psychology. There is enough difference between the theoretical orientation of social psychologists trained in psychology and those trained in sociology that when both groups mutually attack a problem both gain, as the following example illustrates.

Social psychologists are interested in personality, which they define as the patterned or typical ways in which an individual relates himself to the world and to other individuals. Else Frenkel-Brunswik and her associates, psychologists with a Freudian background, found that individuals with strong anti-Semitic attitudes also had anti-Negro attitudes and were rigid, compulsive, and overconforming in their personalities. They called this personality type "the authoritarian personality."

Sociologists were much interested in these findings because they confirmed and gave an explanation for the results of *social distance* [1] tests which showed that highly prejudiced individuals would extend their prejudices even to imaginary groups. Sociologists raised some further questions. Do some kinds of families or some kinds of child-raising habits produce more authoritarian personalities than do others? Since the individual with an authoritarian personality overconforms, he must be conforming to a society which values prejudice. If the society values equality, the overconforming individual should overvalue equality. Is there, then, a differential value on prejudice in different parts of the society? Subsequent research by both psychologists and sociologists seems to show that some lower-class families in the United States do produce more individuals with authoritarian personalities. Since the same group tends to value prejudice, this explains why anti-Semitism and anti-Negro feelings are closely associated with this personality type.

SOCIOLOGY IS DIVIDED INTO SEVERAL SUBFIELDS

The two main theoretical fields of sociology are Social Organization and Social Psychology.

Social Organization or Social Structure

As might be expected in a science which studies group behavior, sociologists, working in one of its two central fields, are preoccupied with classifying and analyzing the structure of groups and studying the relations among them. Although incomplete, for reasons of space, the following list suggests the kinds of groups and relationships and some of their characteristics that interest sociologists:

1. *Institutions:* relatively permanent groups present in almost all societies, like the family, the army, a school, or an industry.

---

[1] See p. 31.

2. *Small, voluntary groups:* groups more ephemeral than institutions; found in some societies much more than in others, like the PTA's, delinquent gangs, bridge clubs, political parties.
3. *Stratified groups:* groups, like castes and classes, whose members have differential amounts of whatever the society values and which, as a result, have differential amounts of power.
4. *Relationships within and among groups:* relationships such as conflict within a political party or between political parties, or the accommodation that results when union and industry representatives sign a contract.
5. *Relationships within and among groups as they are affected by the environment:* as the effect of a rural or suburban environment on the family or the school system.

Having said that sociologists are interested in groups, the writer must immediately qualify this statement. To the layman, "the family" probably calls up a picture of mother, father, and two children setting off together for a picnic or to church. A sociologist will mentally translate "the family" into another phrase, "a cluster of interrelated roles." To the layman this is gibberish. To the sociologist it is clarification. As a radiologist is interested not in the skin and flesh that clothe the body but in the internal structure his X rays reveal, so the sociologist is not interested in the concrete manifestations of family life, but in reaching, with his conceptual tools, what it is in the family that is "social."

Probably everybody today is aware that to a physicist a table is not a solid, substantial support for the dinner one eats off it, but a whirling mass of billions of electrified particles, moving in regular and recurrent patterns. Every educated person grants the physicist the right to look at the dining room table in this way and understands that he is concerned with basic units and processes which explain the structure of all matter and not just the matter of the dining room table. In exactly the same way the sociologist seeks basic social units and processes whose properties and relations explain group behavior in general.

In some groups, like the family or the army, the members mutually adjust their behavior by communicating and interacting with each other. From the point of view of how group members relate to each other, the family and the army, although superficially dissimilar, are basically the same. In sociological jargon, they are *integrated groups.* An integrated group is one of the basic units sociologists work with. *Social processes* are other basic sociological units. Within a family, there is often conflict—among siblings, for example. Within the larger society, conflict occurs between labor and business or among political parties. Sociologists have discovered that conflict is a social process that can be studied in and of itself no matter where it occurs. What is learned about the causes of conflict and its resolution in the family can be applied equally precisely to political conflict.

Social Psychology

One of the subdivisions of the second important theoretical field of sociology, social psychology, is called *collective behavior*—the study of the behavior of individuals in *nonintegrated groups*. *Crowds, audiences,* and *publics* are examples of nonintegrated groups, and their distinguishing characteristic is that their members do not communicate with one another.

The primary concern of social psychology, however, has to do with how the individual and the group are related. A baby is an animal with only the potentialities of becoming a human being. If a baby is deprived of contact with human beings it does not become human, as studies of abandoned, neglected, rejected, or isolated, but mentally normal, children show. An adult deprived of human contact will cease to exhibit human traits. An individual who is mentally ill is either totally or in part nonhuman, depending on the severity of his illness. These are the most basic and best substantiated facts in sociology, and they apply everywhere in the world.

What is it that makes human beings human? Obviously, it cannot be something that grows spontaneously and inevitably in the individual since it develops only when the individual is in a group. It must be something that joins the individual to other members of a group, but just as obviously it is not something concrete and visible like a bridge which joins an island to the mainland.

To answer these questions, social psychologists postulate (that is, invent and name) a quality in the individual which can be developed only by communication and interaction with other group members. This quality they call the *social self*. The ways in which this self is developed they call *socialization*. The social self is not tangible. It is not located in the liver or the brain. It is not synonymous with the concept of personality mentioned a few pages back. It is much less than the total individual. One of the main tasks of social psychologists is to give form and shape to this elusive abstraction, the social self, and to explain its genesis and development.

History of Sociology

In order to avoid the mistakes of their predecessors, sociologists study the history of their science. An interesting and fruitful subdivision of this field is the *sociology of knowledge.* Law; science; literature and the other arts; and political, economic, and religious ideologies are all products of group life and can, therefore, be studied in the same way as can other products of group life. With the same techniques one uses to study why the child-rearing techniques of American middle-class families have become "permissive," one can also study why American sociologists of the thirties were preoccupied with social change in contrast to sociologists in the sixties, who are more concerned with consensus or agreement in society.

Social Problems

Individuals frequently enter sociology because they are interested in social problems and want to find solutions for them.[2] The field of social problems has always been a large and lively one, but its content has undergone much change. Crime is always with us; one of the few enduring divisions within the field of social problems is *criminology. Medical sociology* is new. Among other things, medical sociologists study the problems of administering large institutions; the relations among the medical professions and between the medical professions and their clienteles; and institutional arrangements that have therapeutic value for both physical and mental disorders. At one time *immigration* was a major interest of sociologists. Today, it is of little concern, but the study of *minority group relations* is important.

Sometimes the study of a social problem starts for a reason which becomes less important as the field grows. *Industrial sociology* was stimulated immediately after World War I by a few large industries interested in weaning workers away from unions. Industrial sociologists today are hired by, and study, unions as well as industries, and the field includes the study of any kind of group behavior within the industrial sector of a society.

---

[2] This statement does not imply that sociologists as a group have any obligation to try to solve social problems. Their commitment is to develop the science of sociology. Whether or not one works in the field of social problems is a matter of taste and interest.

Changes in the content of the field mirror changes in the society. When a problem is solved, or when a society is not interested in solving the problem, sociologists generally do not study it. This is not only because sociologists reflect the concerns of the society of which they are a part but also because sociological research is expensive. Only when society regards a situation as both undesirable and susceptible to change is there enough money and institutional support to pursue the study of the problem adequately.

The field of social problems should not be regarded as parallel to the fields of social structure and social psychology. It is, rather, a large laboratory in which the basic theory of sociology is developed, tested, and applied. Medicine could not have found the cause and cure of polio by studying only its symptoms. It was necessary to study epidemiology, virology, and serology. Similarly, juvenile vandalism or race riots are symptoms of social problems, and to understand and cure them it is necessary to study social structure and social psychology. A large part of sociological theory has been developed by studying social problems, just as knowledge of the nature of viruses was increased by studying polio. There have always been some sociologists who deprecate the study of social problems and advise sociologists to concentrate on "pure" research. They say that only when basic theory is completely understood will we have enough knowledge to solve social problems. This is perhaps like trying to find the causes of polio without ever seeing a polio patient!

Population or Demography

The study of the growth and distribution of human populations (*population* or *demography*) is a separate science which historically has been taught in departments of sociology in the United States. Demography becomes important to sociologists when they study the kind of problem discussed below.

Since World War II the average life expectancy of people reaching the age of sixty has been extended by various medical advances. What does it mean to the individual who lives long past this age in a society which is not prepared to take care of him? This is one of the questions which interest sociologists. Before they could begin to analyze the effects of an increase in the aged, sociologists would need to know how many people of each sex there are in the over-sixty age group; how much income and education they have; what religion they profess; where they live; what proportion of the total population they represent; and how these factors have changed over a given time span. It takes special techniques to collect these data accurately, and sociologists turn to demographers for them.

METHODS OF RESEARCH

All sociologists must understand research methodology. Some sociologists devote the bulk of their time to developing and testing new research instruments and processes. Because of its importance, Chapter 3 is devoted entirely to *methodology*.

In these few pages, I have tried to indicate the kinds of situations and events that arouse the curiosity of sociologists and stimulate them to speculation and research. The careful reader should also have become aware that sociologists have their own "perspective"; that is, when they are acting as sociologists, they view the world in a specialized way. The next chapter tells of the development of sociology and will try to show how this peculiar perspective developed.

Some Important Developments in Sociology

chapter two

THE INTERNATIONAL CHARACTER OF SOCIOLOGY

Sociology received its name and its purpose—the scientific study of society—from a Frenchman, Auguste Comte (1798–1847). The name, however, preceded the fact, and sociology could not be regarded as a science until sociologists were able to define a field of study and to devise empirical methods to investigate it. Sociology emerged at the end of the nineteenth century almost simultaneously in Europe (in France, Germany, and Italy) and in the United States. During this period many American sociologists completed their education in Europe. They brought home the theories of the great French sociologists, Emile Durkheim (1855–1917) Gabriel Tarde (1843–1904) and Gustav Le Bon (1841–1931); and, from Germany, the theories of Max Weber (1864–1920) and Georg Simmel (1858–1918). Thus, from the very beginning sociology has had an international character.

Despite its auspicious beginning, sociology in Europe has developed in an inconsistent fashion. Only in France has sociology had both an early start and continual growth, resulting today in chairs in all the leading universities, a rich variety of sociological schools and theoretical approaches, and a brilliant roster of names. German sociology, one of the most fruitful in the world, was destroyed by Hitler. There is now only a feeble development in Germany. A flourishing school of sociology in Italy was seriously weakened under Fascism and is just beginning to revive. There was a small development in Finland, started by E. A. Westermarck (1862–1939), and another in Poland, originating in the work of Florian Znaniecki (1882–1958). Poland has managed to maintain its sociological traditions through war and dictatorships, something other countries in a similar position have been unable to do.

In 1949 UNESCO stimulated and provided financial support for a meeting in Oslo to found the *International Sociological Association* (ISA). The first full-fledged meeting of the ISA was held in Zurich in 1950 and was attended by 100 delegates from a score of countries. Since that time, meetings have been held at regular intervals. The latest—the 1962 session in Washington, D.C. —was attended by over 1,000 delegates. This figure alone indicates the significant expansion of sociology in only twelve years.

In addition to the assistance, stimulation, and inspiration scholars receive from each other, international communication among sociologists is important in a more direct way to the future of this field. Sociologists hope to find universal laws of human behavior. Some sociologists hold that this is impossible because most human behavior is culture-bound. Until now there has been little opportunity for sociologists—unlike anthropologists—to do the comparative studies that would furnish proof on one side or the other. The programs of the ISA are always centered around a main subject and are announced three years ahead of time. This encourages sociologists from different countries to concentrate their research in the field which will be examined at the next international meeting. As a result, the *Proceedings of the World Congresses* provide a series of comparative studies about modern society never before available.

Sociology is now studied in all European countries except, perhaps, Portugal and Albania. Japan, Israel, Egypt, Turkey, and India have a number of sociologists; and the work in Japan and Israel is often first rate. Sociological study is going on in South and Central American countries, and Brazil and Mexico have some strength in the field. The leading political opponent of Prime Minister Nkrumah in Ghana was K. A. Busia, an English-trained sociologist, now in exile. Sociology is beginning in New Zealand and Australia.

It is a tribute to the accomplishments of American sociologists that sociology has been called "the American science." As the preceding paragraphs show, this is an exaggeration, but sociology has developed more rapidly in the United States than else-where. Students and professors have traveled back and forth between Canadian and American universities to study and teach.

Thus, sociology in Canada has developed simultaneously and co-operatively with that in the United States.

THE ABANDONMENT OF SINGLE-CAUSE, DETERMINIST THEORIES OF SOCIAL BEHAVIOR

Such a capsule history does not reveal how sociology moved from a wish to study society to a science capable of explaining a great deal about social life. What follows is a description of some of the important discoveries that shaped modern sociology.

A striking trend in sociology has been the progressive abandonment of monistic (one-cause), determinist theories of social behavior. These theories assume that social behavior is shaped and controlled by one powerful and impersonal force, like heredity or economic conditions or culture.

In the late nineteenth and early twentieth centuries, biology, particularly in the field of genetics, made spectacular strides. The excitement engendered by these advances permeated all intellectual life, and many sociologists were seduced into attributing variations in social behavior to hereditary differences. Lombroso and his followers believed that criminals inherited their "criminal nature" and that they could be distinguished from other people by the size of their heads or the shape of their ear lobes. Others believed that mental illness was inherited. In the United States anti-immigration laws were supported by statements of sociologists that some national groups were so different in heredity from the population already here that they could never be assimilated. These arguments, used first against the Chinese and next against the Irish, were applied to each successive wave of immigrants—the Scandinavians, Central Europeans, and, finally, the Italians. The same arguments were used to oppose labor legislation and slum clearance. The lower classes, it was said, were biologically inferior, and no legal changes could improve their condition.[1]

Other sociologists refuted biological determinism. They pointed out that the heredity make-up of a population is constant, whereas social behavior changes rapidly. For example: criminals reform,

---

[1] One of the most notorious studies of this kind compares two family histories—that of the Jukes and that of the Kallikaks. The Jukes supposedly exhibited every possible kind of moral and social deviation generation after generation, while the Kallikaks were all model citizens. Later investigators found that practically none of the family members had been interviewed or traced to the original progenitors. This study is mentioned because it is still often found in outdated secondary texts.

the mentally ill recover, the children of illiterate immigrants become doctors and lawyers, and the lower classes move rapidly into the middle class. Studies of criminals showed that, as a group, they did not differ from the noncriminal population in appearance, intelligence, or temperament.

Although biological or hereditary determinism has no scientific standing whatsoever today, it is still accepted among laymen, particularly in the form of racism. The same kind of empirical evidence that destroyed the credibility of biological determinism as a cause of criminality is available to disprove various aspects of racism. For example: Southern Negro children who migrate North exhibit an increase in their I.Q. scores. Northern-educated Negroes score higher on army intelligence tests, on the average, than do Southern-educated whites. There are many cases of Negro children with high I.Q.'s, some as high as 200. None of these things would be possible if intelligence were linked with race. Many other studies could be cited to show that no racial group has a monopoly on any kind of social behavior, good or bad.[2]

As research demonstrated fallacies in biological determinism, many social scientists began to attribute the causes of social behavior entirely to the influence of the environment, particularly the economic environment. Economic determinism springs from the ideas of Karl Marx and is widely accepted, although many businessmen would blanch upon being told that some of their theories of social behavior bear a resemblance to Marxist theories. The belief that a capitalistic economic system can solve all problems is as much economic determinism as the persuasion that socialism will cure all the world's ills. Some sociologists, particularly in Europe, analyzed society in Marxist terms. Others developed more specific and narrower theories.

In 1929 William Fielding Ogburn (1886–1959) was asked by President Hoover to direct a study of social change. Published under the title of *Recent Social Trends* (1930–1933), the study provides a wealth of accurate, statistical information about the United States in the period following World War I, but its theory

---

[2] For refutations of biological determinism, see: Charles Horton Cooley, "Genius, Fame and the Comparison of Race," *Annals of the American Academy of Political and Social Science*, IX (May 1897), 317–58; Franz Boas, *The Mind of Primitive Man* (New York: The Macmillan Co., 1911); Abraham Myerson, *The Inheritance of Mental Diseases* (Baltimore: The Williams & Wilkins Co., 1925); Otto Klineberg, *Race Differences* (New York: Harper & Row, Publishers, 1935). Notice the dates on these references; they were deliberately chosen to show how long it sometimes takes for a theory to die even after it is scientifically refuted.

is an example of economic determinism. Ogburn pivoted the study around the idea that, although technological change is constantly occurring, in an industrial society there is often a lag between technological change and the adaptation of society to the new technology—i.e., a *culture lag.*

Causal explanations of this sort are still common. One hears over and over that automation is causing unemployment. If this is so, why is it that in the USSR and other European countries automation does not cause unemployment? In Russia if an industry is automated the government shifts the displaced labor to another sector of the economy—something our belief in individual freedom prevents our government from doing. In many European countries, the government manipulates the economy to provide a slight inflation to stimulate industrial expansion and absorb excess labor. Similar solutions have been slow of acceptance in the United States. Until recently, technological unemployment fell most heavily on minority groups. Relatively few citizens have cared enough to accept the higher taxes necessary to retrain minority group workers. The cause of unemployment in an increasingly auto- mated society, then, is not the oversimplified culture lag, but a complicated interplay of American attitudes toward government, economics, and race.

Formerly, economic determinism was accepted as the cause of the class structure of our society and as the reason for discrimi- nation against minority groups. Research has shown the causes of both phenomena to be more complex. At one time it was assumed that broken homes, poverty, and disorganized neighborhoods (used as indices of economic factors) were responsible for juvenile delinquency, illegitimacy, adult crimes, unemployability, the prob- lems of old age, and even mental deficiency and mental illness. When, however, studies showed that many individuals subject to these influences did not exhibit problem behavior and that many of those who did misbehave came from economically satisfactory backgrounds, the economic determinist theories were weakened.

Max Weber, a German sociologist, was highly influential in discrediting economic determinism. He did a series of monographs on the influence of religious ideas on the rest of social life, the best known of which is *The Protestant Ethic and The Spirit of Capitalism.* He showed that the rise of Protestantism (particularly Calvinism with its emphasis on individual rights and responsi- bilities) not only preceded modern European capitalism in time but provided an extremely congenial atmosphere for its growth. Weber's brilliant analysis of the effect of ideologies on the economic structure of societies played an important part in turning sociology away from economic determinism.

Monistic deterministic theories were also expressed in *social determinism* or *cultural determinism.* Social determinism has yielded some lasting concepts, although its point of view has been abandoned. The chief exponent of social determinism was William Graham Sumner (1840–1910), one of the earliest American sociologists. Sumner exemplifies a school of sociology called Social Darwinism, after Charles Darwin, creator of the theory of evolution. At one time this was a leading school of sociological thought, boasting such names as Herbert Spencer (1820–1903) in England and Lester Ward (1841–1913) in the United States.

The Folkways, Sumner's major work, is a study of *social control*—the ways in which a social group inculcates the values of the group into the minds of its members and prevents deviant behavior, producing common agreement or *consensus.* When social control and consensus break down, revolution and reorganization of the society occur. Nobody knows how much consensus a society needs to function, but this is one of the central concerns of sociologists today. Sumner thought of the operation of social control as automatic and inevitable and believed that the individual was completely formed and controlled by the operation of "natural" social laws. This is what is meant by social determinism.

Social determinism was not as easy to refute as biological and economic determinisms had been, but it, too, yielded to analysis. The following sections show how and why sociologists have finally abandoned all monistic, deterministic theories.

THE SEARCH FOR VALID GENERALIZATIONS

Sociologists have abandoned single-cause theories because they find that both the causes and effects of social behavior are very complex. For example, today many married women are going to work when their children are half grown. The involved myriad of events that precipitated the large-scale return of married women to work developed over a long period of time. The idea that women are not biologically inferior to men and should have equal political and economic rights has been gaining acceptance for a hundred years. This is an ideological factor. Another factor is the availability of methods to limit family size. The invention of birth control techniques is a technological change. Their acceptance is an ideological change. There are other causative factors such as the movement of large groups of people into the middle class so that a second salary becomes necessary to maintain the desired standard of living. Women have been freer to work outside the home since the invention of low-cost, processed foods and labor-saving devices for the home. This series of interrelated changes is certainly not the result of the working of any single, immutable, "natural" law— biological, economic, or cultural.

Many social institutions are being affected by the movement of married women into the labor force, and there will be effects in the future on which we can only speculate at this time. For example, many women are going into teaching because it has traditionally been a woman's profession and because the hours of work coincide with the hours when their children are away from home. An influx of mature married women into the teaching profession can affect both the teaching profession and the structure of the educational system. Mothers experienced in raising children may well challenge current educational theories and practice with an assurance younger trainees could not have. Teachers have traditionally submitted tamely to low wages and community control of their behavior, in part because most of them were single women entirely dependent on their salaries. Married women, whose earn- ings constitute a second family salary and whose community status is established, can afford to be more independent.

There have been predictions that when mothers work outside the home there will be an increase of divorce and juvenile delinquency. The evidence about an increase of divorce is unclear, but studies show that there is little relation between juvenile delinquency and the working mother.

As more women move into the labor force, we can expect an increase in the purchase of processed food and ready-made clothing, of labor-saving devices for the home, and of second family automo- biles. Voluntary associations like the PTA, the Girl Scouts, the Red Cross, and political clubs are finding it more difficult to recruit leadership. The working woman does not have time for much volunteer activity.

Similarly any social event is both the result of a multiplicity of causes and itself a contributing cause to other social events. *In sociological terms all the institutions of a society and its culture are interrelated over time.* Sociologists are not only interested in the interrelationships among institutions. They are also concerned about how any change affects society as a whole. How, for example, do the changes in women's roles affect consensus?

At one time in the United States, there was consensus that a woman should stay at home and be a good wife and mother. Most people agreed on this, and there was little behavior deviating from this value. Today, some people disapprove of married women working. Others accept it. In certain circles women are being urged not to waste their talents and education on housework when they have no small children. There is thus much less consensus about the role of married women than there was fifty years ago. Different parts of the society are inculcating different values.

Is it possible to find a sociological generalization that will do justice to multiple causation, explain the interrelationships of institutions, and deal with society as a whole at the same time? Such generalizations are rare, but there are some.

The Theory of the Division of Labor

One of the generalizations or laws adequate to explain the complexity of society is the *division of labor*. In 1893 Emile Durkheim published *The Division of Labor in Society*, developing therein the division of labor concept which has proved useful in analyzing both *consensus* and *stratification*.

A modern industrial society is characterized by a multiplicity of occupational groups—teachers, doctors, shoemakers, public relations experts, civil servants, astronauts, garbage collectors, and others. Because the work of each group is specialized, everyone in the society is highly dependent upon everyone else. The society as a whole can continue only when each group carries out its occupational tasks. Mutual dependence of groups holds modern societies together (creates consensus).

On the other hand, the work one does leads to differences in income, education, prestige, and attitudes toward the world. Sociologists say that the society is *stratified*. Sometimes they call this kind of society *pluralistic*. Does the division of labor mean then that one's loyalties belong first to the occupational group and only secondly to the larger society? Is the mutual economic dependence of groups more compelling than the mutual antagonisms that develop out of different world views? When a labor union in a basic industry threatens to go on strike or a basic industry raises its prices, these questions assume practical importance. Exclusive loyalty to one's profession may also spring from the division of labor. Physicians in Belgium in April, 1964, angered at government regulation of their profession, went on strike and refused to treat any but the most critically ill. Eventually, the government had to draft doctors into the army to avoid complete panic and collapse of the society. Similarly, on the basis of the division of labor theory, we might ask what are the consequences for the society of confining one group to menial occupations, as has been done to Negroes in the United States?

In a pluralistic society, people are exposed to world views different from their own. Does this lead them to harden their own views? Does it make them more tolerant? Does it weaken every point of view so that none survives? If this happens, does the society collapse or does a new and common *ideology* (set of beliefs and values) emerge? These are questions of consensus for which sociologists are trying to find adequate answers. One approach is to examine in detail the ways in which a group inculcates and enforces group values on the group members (social control).

The Relationship Between the Individual and the Group

In the process of abandoning determinism of all kinds, sociologists learned that men's behavior is influenced at one and the same time by their biological structure, the functioning of their minds, the kind of culture they are a part of, their relations with others, their past experiences, the kinds of groups they participate in, and the particular circumstances of an act. Many sociologists began to conceive of men *acting within a social structure.* Their behavior is not determined; men choose their behavior. Herbert Blumer describes this point of view:

> Instead of the individual being surrounded by an environment of pre-existing objects which play upon him and call forth his behavior, the proper picture is that he constructs his objects on the basis of his on-going activity. . . . His behavior, accordingly, is not a result of such things as environmental pressures, stimuli, motives, attitudes and ideas, but arises instead from how he interprets and handles these things in the action which he is now constructing.[3]

When the construction of an action by an individual is analyzed further, the following facts emerge:

1. Each individual is unique.
2. Nevertheless, some individuals behave similarly. New Yorkers behave more like each other than they do like Romans. Most men act more like other men than like women.

---

[3] "Society as Symbolic Interaction," in Arnold M. Rose (ed.), *Human Behavior and Social Processes* (Boston: Houghton Mifflin Co., 1962), pp. 182–83.

3. Individuals occupying different positions in society behave differently, and individuals behave differently at different times. A business executive behaves differently than a coal miner. Both of them behave differently toward their children than they do to their co-workers or their ministers, although they may behave differently from each other in each of these relations.
4. Society is always changing. Each generation wonders what the next is coming to.
5. On the other hand, groups exhibit continuity. They have traditions that are passed on from generation to generation.

An adequate theory of social behavior must explain both change and stability, both unique and common behavior, and how individuals relate to the other members of the group. To account for individuality and uniqueness, sociologists postulate, as one part of the social self,[4] something they call the *I*. Like the self, the I does not really exist. It is a concept sociologists have invented. Common observation shows that no two individuals, even identical twins, behave exactly alike. No two women mother their children in exactly the same way, although they may agree entirely on how children should be raised. No two teachers teach in exactly the same manner, even though they have been teaching the same subject in the same school for the same length of time, have been professionally trained in the same department of education, and agree on what should be taught and how to teach it. Whatever it is within the self that constructs behavior uniquely for each individual (and we do not know what it is at present) is subsumed under the term, the I.

Similarly, in order to explain the fact that people frequently act alike, sociologists assume that the self contains reflections of what the group or society expects. These expectations are called *me's*. When the me's are related and cluster together, they are called *roles*. All the expectations society has of how women should behave constitute the role of women. As we have said earlier, people live in groups and they therefore learn, in a variety of ways, how other members of the group expect them to behave in certain circumstances. Each person internalizes (integrates into the self structure) the expectations of the groups he belongs to. This explains why members of the same group behave alike and why members of different groups behave differently. For example, it explains why teachers behave more like other teachers than they do like salesmen.

---

[4] See pp. 6–7.

Why have sociologists been concerned with mapping out the internal structure of the self? For one thing, they can thus explain why social control works. An individual will not respond to social controls, like gossip or prison or the awarding of public esteem, unless his social self contains the appropriate expectations or me's. Threats that the high-school drop-out will receive low wages or face unemployment will fall on deaf ears unless the student feels that steady employment and a high income are desirable.[5] A woman who belongs to a group that does not frown on illegitimacy, although most other groups in a society do, is likely to produce illegitimate children even though the larger society punishes her.

From the point of view of the larger society, anything which blocks the internalization of expectations for a large group of people is important to study. Isolation of a group, whatever its cause, results in the group members learning different kinds of expectations than most of us do. The Southerner who practices segregation today, the rural Negro male who does not fulfill his paternal role, the lower-class slum child who rejects what the school wants to teach him, many American Indian tribes who try to live as their ancestors did, the mentally ill—all of these groups behave in ways not consonant with the expectations of the majority of Americans. Their behavior can only be changed by directing proper expectations toward them in situations in which they can internalize the expectations. This requires knowing how social expectations are acquired—a process studied under the name of socialization.

Change, as well as isolation, can also result in a failure of social control. When a social catastrophe occurs—war or revolution or rapid social change resulting in unemployment—the individual finds that the behavior society once expected of him (which he has internalized or learned) is either no longer possible or does not bring social approval. When a man cannot find work, he may no longer be respected and looked up to by his family and neighbors. He knows society expects him to work. He wants to work but he cannot. He becomes bewildered, sometimes apathetic, sometimes mentally ill, and sometimes anti-social. Retired people are often in this situation because a lifetime of hard work has brought them neither economic security nor prestige. Social control fails because the fulfillment of social expectations is unrewarding. In a society whose population is increasing and enjoying a progressively higher standard of living and education, those who rise

---

[5] He may, of course, just not believe the threats will materialize, but that is a separate problem.

socially and economically may not have internalized the expectations relevant to their new situation. They may not know, for example, how to motivate their children to want a higher education. When a great many groups in a society find that the expectations directed toward them are impossible to fulfill or when they do not understand what the expectations are because of isolation or change, social controls fail and consensus breaks down.

This chapter has not been, in the main, a conventional history of sociology. By showing some of the false roads sociology has followed and then forsaken, the author has tried to help the reader avoid these unrewarding paths. It is hoped that the exposition of some of the complexities of social life has made clear why sociologists have created abstract and difficult concepts. Modern sociologists are face to face with the difficult task of studying very complex phenomena, parts of which are concealed inside the minds of individuals. This condition has affected not only their approach and the kind of concepts they invent, but also the way in which they interpret and apply scientific method. The next chapter will explore the methodology of sociology.

The Methods Employed by Sociologists   chapter three

OBSTACLES TO SOCIOLOGICAL RESEARCH

The nature of the material social scientists study creates problems that natural scientists do not have. If an amoeba is unhappy about having its private life bared to the world, the biologist does not know this. If he did, he probably would not care. Social scientists are, however, restricted in their ability to observe all aspects of human behavior.

Sexual life is private. Many people are reluctant to reveal their financial status, police records, or other situations which shame and embarrass them. Even if an informant thinks he is answering a questionnaire truthfully, he may not be. Men have a great capacity for deceiving themselves. When a man's reasons for thinking or doing something lie in his unconscious mind, they are accessible to the researcher only by special techniques.

In our society a sociologist can experiment with human beings only to a limited degree and only with their permission. The use of cameras and recording devices without the knowledge or consent of the people being studied creates situations in which invasion of privacy and blackmail may result. Both psychologists and sociologists have recently attempted to formulate codes of ethics which forbid observing people without their prior permission. Knowledge of our own behavior tells us, however, that when people know they are being observed they are not likely to behave exactly as they would if they thought no one was about. Even the observation of public life is often restricted. When one sociologist, for example, wanted to place a recording machine in a jury room to find out how decisions were reached, the courts forbade it.

Finally, a social scientist studies creatures like himself. With some of them he may share experiences, attitudes, and values. Others may engage in behavior which he abhors. Like other men, the social scientist may not be completely aware of his own attitudes or know that some of them are determined in his unconscious.

In the face of all the peculiar circumstances that surround the study of society, sociologists have had to be sure that it was *possible* to have a science of social behavior. A part of every sociologist's professional training is a study of *what* conditions have to be met in order to have a science. He is also taught a variety of ways of preventing, or at least minimizing, the intrusion of his own values into his scientific studies.

HOW A SOCIOLOGIST DOES HIS WORK

It is often stated, and probably widely believed, that a scientist starts by observing the facts. A little reflection will show that this is impossible. Which facts? There are billions of facts in the world. Nobody can ever observe them all—certainly not a sociologist setting out to do a small piece of research in a limited area. The first thing a scientist has to do is to decide what he is going to study. The kind of scientist he is determines this in part. An endocrinologist is unlikely to be interested in volcanic structure. Similarly, a sociologist is unlikely to be interested in the rate of death of a dying star. He is going to be interested in social behavior of some kind.

More than likely he will be interested in only a limited area of human behavior. Because very few men can learn much about all human behavior, sociologists, like other scientists, specialize. Most sociologists are competent in more than one field, but few are competent in more than several fields. A sociologist may consider himself a social psychologist, an expert in minority group relations, and an urban sociologist. He may never work in industrial sociology or rural sociology or medical sociology. Specialization probably increases a sociologist's efficiency, but it also narrows his vision. Many motives help determine what kind of research interests a sociologist. Let us follow a sociologist who is a specialist in minority group relations as he goes about doing a piece of research to see how he works and why he picks a particular area to work in. The time is early in 1960.

Hopefully, our man (we shall call him Professor X) does not start his project with a blank mind. It is filled not only with the same kind of knowledge other people of his age and experience have, but also with sociological theories[1] about minority groups. Among other things he would have the following information in his mind:

1. A *minority group* is a group of people who are aware of themselves as a group and who meet some discrimination from other groups in the society. In the United States minority groups include Jews, Negroes, Indians, Orientals, Catholics, and others.

2. All groups, including minority groups, have *morale*. That is, their members have common values and are able to work together to achieve group goals.

3. Sometimes group morale is high, sometimes low. Both high and low morale are reflected in the behavior of group members.

4. Minority groups with high morale support their own members when possible.

This information lies dormant in Professor X's mind until one day when he gets into a discussion with a colleague on whether Republican Catholics are going to support John F. Kennedy, a Democrat, in the 1960 election because he is a Catholic.

Professor X sees the upcoming election as an opportunity to do some research. His motives are many and complex:

1. The study of group morale has been very fashionable lately and some of the research has stimulated Professor X to formulate some ideas of his own. He is aware that a study of group morale would be easily publishable, although this is probably not a major motive.

2. Professor X is professionally almost as much interested in political behavior as he is in minority groups. He has already formulated his ideas about group morale in political terms. He has undoubtedly taken into consideration the fact that this research will be simplified procedurally and financially if he can set up his study so that election returns can be used.

3. Some of Professor X's values add weight to his interest in doing the study. He is disturbed that the religious issue has been injected into the campaign and is unhappy that there is a possibility of bloc voting.

---

[1] Theories are nothing but systematic and detailed explanations of some portion of reality. In Chapter 2 we discussed the theory of the division of labor, for example. Theories, by the way, are very easy to think up. Proving them is the difficult thing.

Acting upon all these motives, Professor X decides to study Catholic voting in the 1960 election. He will, of course, need some money to do the study, and he decides to ask for it from a foundation that has funds available for research. The foundation will naturally want to know what this study will add to scientific knowledge before it gives away money, so Professor X writes out a proposal in which he explains the purpose of his research.

Professor X has decided that if Republican Catholics vote for Kennedy in large numbers, this would be an example of the effects of high group morale in a religious minority group. He writes down everything he knows about group morale which has been discovered by past studies and which is generally accepted by other sociologists as an explanation (theory) of group morale. This includes, among other things, what morale is, what kinds of situations produce high morale, how high group morale affects the behavior of individual group members, and so on. He ends this part of his proposal with a hypothesis.[2]

A hypothesis is a tentative prediction. The first part of the hypothesis starts with the word *if* and says *if this theory is true*; the second part starts with *then* and says *then we can expect to find this kind of behavior*. Professor X's hypothesis might read: If a minority group has high morale, then its members will support a member under attack.

His next step is to translate his hypothesis into something he can study. A translation of his hypothesis might read: Catholics are a minority group with high morale and will, therefore, vote for Kennedy in greater proportion than they did for previous Democratic Presidential candidates because Kennedy is under attack for his Catholicism.

Professor X still has to explain how he is going to do his research. One of the first problems is to locate a group of Catholics to study. Religious affiliation is not asked by the U.S. *Census*, so he cannot look there. He might look in a city telephone directory to find the location of Catholic churches. Most Catholic churches are neighborhood churches, so that one could assume that wherever there is a Catholic church there are Catholics living in the area. One could not assume, however, that most people in the neighborhood are Catholic. Civic leaders or heads of public agencies would probably be able to tell Professor X the areas of a city in which many people of Mexican, Italian, Irish, or Polish

---

[2] This is a simplification. If Professor X really expected to get any money, he would have to present half a dozen hypotheses. They would be in the same form as the one we are presenting.

descent live. Most of them are likely to be Catholic, and they frequently (but not always) live in separate neighborhoods.

Professor X, however, would not want to study these big-city groups, because they usually vote Democratic. If they were to vote for Kennedy, it could not be assumed that they had done so because both he and they were Catholic. Rather Professor X would look for an area in which most of the inhabitants are Catholic and habitually vote Republican. He could then study changes in their voting behavior from 1952 and 1956, when there was no Catholic Presidential candidate, to 1960 when there was. He would try to find a rural, Catholic, Republican county. Again, he would have to look for traditionally Catholic nationality groups who have settled in rural areas.

He would also like to find more than one area to study since local conditions might affect voting behavior in a single area. Voters might, for example, shift to the Democratic ticket in reaction to a poor, local Republican administration or to a local problem such as high unemployment, rather than because they identify with Kennedy as a Catholic.

Professor X also has to offer some way of proving that the Catholics he studies have high morale. He may have available descriptions of the past history of the counties which indicate this, or he may decide to do a questionnaire survey of community leaders and/or a sample of the residents, or he may use both techniques. This also goes into the proposal.

Professor X gets his money. He builds a questionnaire designed to find out if the Catholics being studied exhibit high group morale. He administers the questionnaire and interprets the findings. They show high group morale among the Catholics. Notice that Professor X has done most of his work on the basis of past knowledge before he has made any field observations at all. After the election he hires a graduate student to compare the votes for Kennedy with the number of votes for the Democratic presidential candidates in 1952 and 1956 in the counties he is studying. He adjusts for population changes and local conditions, tests to see if the difference is significant,[3] and comes to the conclusion that Catholics *did* vote more heavily for the Catholic, Democratic, Presidential candidate in 1960 then they had in 1952 and 1956. He feels justified in concluding that this does indicate that a minority group with high group morale will demonstrate it by supporting one of their members under attack for belonging to the minority group. Sociological theories about bloc voting as an indication of high minority group

---

[3] This is a technical term which indicates that the results of a statistical analysis have not occurred by chance alone.

morale have been strengthened. They cannot be proved, however, with one study. Before they can be regarded as proved, they must be tested by a large number of similar cases of minority group behavior. At some point sociologists can use this theory to predict behavior. They can say with assurance how minority groups would vote under specified circumstances. *The ability to predict accurately is the aim of all science.* It should be noted that if Professor X had found that Catholics did not vote heavily for Kennedy, this would have been just as important to science because it would have shown the theory to be wrong in some respect.

Research Techniques

The research techniques sociologists use may be no more complicated than those Professor X used. When necessary, however, difficult and complicated mathematical and statistical techniques may be employed. The researcher may gather his data by questionnaire or interview. Questionnaires can be designed to get at unconscious attitudes and motives. They are called *projective tests* because they are constructed in such a way that unconscious elements are projected into the responses. Interviews may be short and guided by a questionnaire, or they may be long and probing— *depth interviews.*

Sociologists sometimes do *content analysis.* That is, they count the number of times words or ideas or stereotypes or attitudes appear in a given context. This technique is used to analyze the mass media (newspapers, TV and radio programs, magazines). It may also be used to analyze fiction, poetry, or even public-school textbooks. Content studies which showed that certain minority groups were inevitably depicted as menials, villains, or fools have done much to change stories in magazines with national circulation. The material in TV advertising and programming has also been altered to give a more realistic portrayal of minorities. It should be added that the studies alone did not produce changes. Militant minorities used the studies to buttress their protests.

An important method in sociology is *historical analysis.* The sociologist goes to the historian for evidence to support his theory. Comparative studies of large groups like city neighborhoods or unions or nations are likely to be based on historical materials. One sociologist studied the history of land values over 100 years in Chicago. Some have studied patterns of migration, and others have compared the development of cities in Europe and America.[4] Whenever an individual or event is representative in most respects of a

---

[4] For other examples of historical analysis, see pp. 2–3 and pp. 15–16.

category of individuals or events, sociologists can make a careful and detailed study of a single case and reasonably generalize from that case to the whole category. Intensive research of this kind is called a *case study*. The detailed history of a garment workers' union local can tell us much about other locals in the same union. Case studies make it easier to compare phenomena, as, for example, a typical garment workers' local with a typical boilermakers' local. Case studies are useful in tracing changes over time; e.g., the stages a business passes through as it moves from one-man ownership to a corporation structure.

One kind of case study is the *life history*—a chronological account of the important events in an individual's life which reveals the experiences and events that have most influenced his behavior. A famous life history—*The Jack Roller* (1930)—recounts the life history of a criminal, through which sociologists hoped to better understand the motives that lead to a criminal career.

Sometimes sociologists take groups into laboratories and conduct *experiments* under controlled conditions. They may try to create group solidarity and high morale in the groups under study and then see if they can be broken down and by what methods. One is never sure, however, that the groups in the laboratory are representative of social groups outside the laboratory. Whenever possible, sociologists prefer to study social groups outside the laboratory—boy scout troops, hospital wards, a union local, a department in a factory, a public-school class. The sociologist who was refused permission to study real juries asked citizens on the official jury lists to serve on mock juries. Once a mock jury was assembled, he presented real cases to them in exactly the same manner as the original cases had been tried in court. Their deliberations were recorded, then studied to see how the mock juries arrived at their decisions. This is not as satisfactory as a study of a real jury. The mock juries, made up of a cross section of citizens, were, however, more like real juries than the usual laboratory groups composed of college students could possibly be.

Sometimes a sociologist will keep careful records of what goes on in a group of which he is a member so that he may study it. Because a sociologist shares the aims and values of any group he belongs to, he may not be objective in his analysis. On the other hand, he has access to the feelings of members of the group outsiders might have difficulty in perceiving. Some groups, like religious sects or criminal gangs, are difficult to study because their activities are secret. At times researchers have pretended to be members of a closed group to find out what went on in the group. Sociologists, for example, have entered prisons and pretended to be criminals.

One member of a team of social psychologists joined a sect that believed in the imminent end of the world and stayed in the group until the appointed day had come and gone in order to find out how the group would react when their beliefs were not fulfilled. This technique of studying groups is called *participant observation.*

One research method peculiar to sociology is the *ideal-type method,* invented by Max Weber. It is a technique for *comparing complex social phenomena.* The technique requires the researcher to construct models of whatever phenomena are being compared. These are perhaps similar to the miniature models a city planner prepares when he is trying to show his client how a reconstructed area of the city will look. All the pieces are in proper proportion and stand in the same place as the completed buildings will stand; but the buildings have no windows or interiors, trees and grass are represented by green paint, and so on. Ideal types, although they are verbal rather than three dimensional, are like the planner's models in that they include only the broad outlines that define the phenomena and neglect the details.

For example, Robert Merton has constructed four ideal types of people in regard to their attitudes toward discrimination and their prejudice against minorities. They are:

1. the unprejudiced nondiscriminator, or all-weather liberal
2. the unprejudiced discriminator, or fair-weather liberal
3. the prejudiced nondiscriminator, or fair-weather illiberal
4. the prejudiced discriminator, or all-weather illiberal

Merton's types are not logical categories but descriptions built out of careful and repeated observations. Only those traits that are always present and causally important are included.

Sociologists use these and many other techniques when they do research, and they may use several procedures in a single study. Anything that works is acceptable, and new methods of research are constantly being discovered and tried out. How to use research techniques, what constitutes good procedure, and under what circumstances one or another method is suitable are learned as a part of professional training. The layman, reading a piece of research, cannot usually judge the value of the techniques. He can, however, observe whether all the steps Professor X went through have been carried out. Frequently, important steps in research procedure are omitted, and the results of the research are then of doubtful value.

Not All Research Is Valuable

Let us examine the work of another sociologist. Professor Y, also an expert in minority group relations, is interested in seeing whether a film to which he has access will reduce prejudice in school children. He secures permission to show the movie to all the fifth-grade children in the public schools of a Midwestern city we shall call Centertown. Before he shows the film, he tests the children to see how much and what kind of prejudice they have against Negro children. It is assumed that tests can indicate prejudice or lack of it and that Professor Y administers them properly. Then he shows the film to one-half of the classes, chosen at random. Afterwards, he tests all the children again for indications of prejudice against Negro children. He finds there has been a significant reduction of prejudice among the children who saw the movie, and only among those children.[5] He concludes that the movie does reduce the expression of race prejudice, at least immediately after the subjects have seen the film. Professor Y's techniques are impeccable, and there is little doubt that he has done what he claims to have done. He has reduced prejudice among those fifth-grade children in Centertown who saw the film; but, because he did not specify any theory as to what causes prejudice or relate the content of the movie to the theory by using an hypothesis, we have no idea of *why* the children lost their prejudice. We would have no indication of whether the movie would work equally well on another group. We cannot generalize. We can make no predictions on the basis of this study.

Imagine that Professor Y had started with one of the generally accepted theories of prejudice: Most white people have little contact with Negroes. They see them only in menial jobs or through derogatory stereotypes in fiction or the mass media. When whites can see Negroes in situations like their own, their prejudice may be reduced. Imagine also that the movie shows middle-class Negro children engaging in the kind of activities usual with middle-class, Midwestern white children. When Midwestern white children who have little direct contact with Negroes see a movie showing Negro children to be much like themselves, then the prejudice of the white children will be reduced. If Professor Y had stated his theory and hypothesis, then the basic theory—that *equal-status contacts* reduce prejudice—would have been strengthened. We would also know that if we want to try to reduce prejudice in the future we should try to increase equal-status contacts, whether by a movie or some other method. Unfortunately, there are far more Professor Y's than

---

[5] The classes which do not see the movie are the *control group*. If the children in these classes had lost some of their prejudice between the first and second times they were tested, the researcher would conclude that something other than the movie had been operating to reduce prejudice.

Professor X's, and research not firmly anchored in theory is very common, even in professional journals.

THEORIES MUST BEGIN SOMEWHERE

So far we have been dealing with research in fields where there is an established body of sociological theory to be refined and made more precise. How does a sociologist proceed when he is a pioneer in the field? He uses his common sense and hopes that he will lay a foundation on which later research can build. In 1928 Emory S. Bogardus published a *social distance scale*. He had asked nearly 2,000 Americans about their attitudes toward forty racial, nationality, and religious groups in the following situations:

1. would admit to close kinship by marriage
2. would admit to a club as personal friends
3. would admit to residence on the same street as neighbors
4. would admit to employment in the same firm or factory
5. would admit to citizenship in the United States
6. would admit as visitors to the United States
7. would exclude from the country

Most of the respondents were willing to admit British, native white Americans, and Canadians to the close intimacy of marriage. The social distance they wished to keep between themselves and these three groups was small. On the other hand, the social distance they wished to keep between themselves and Negroes, Japanese, Jews, Chinese, Hindus, and Turks was large. Sometimes they did not even want them to enter the country. Other groups, like the French, Spaniards, and Italians, were kept at an intermediate social distance.

Bogardus had no theory except the common-sense observation that some groups in the United States were more discriminated against than others. His social scale was so ingenious and useful a measure of discrimination, however, that many students of discrimination began using it and developing variations of it. Sociologists were surprised to find that Negroes, Jews, Chinese, and Japanese also wished to keep the same social distance between themselves and other groups, except that Negroes accepted Negroes, Jews preferred Jews, and so on. Sociologists had hypothesized that minority groups would show less prejudice. They then developed the theory that prejudice is part of American culture and that minority groups learn it just as the majority group does. This gradual accumulation of research around a narrow subject, each study reinforcing and refining the theory, is the way basic theory is built.[6]

One of the results of wishing to keep social distance between one's self and others is discrimination. In the United States discrimination is much sharper in some areas than in others. Gunnar Myrdal, in *An American Dilemma*,[7] postulated a *rank order of discrimination*. The white man's rank order of discrimination is as follows:

Rank 1. The bar against intermarriage and sexual intercourse involving white women.

Rank 2. The discrimination against equality in social relations, such as dancing, swimming, eating, or drinking together.

Rank 3. Discrimination in the use of public facilities, such as schools and churches.

Rank 4. Political disfranchisement.

Rank 5. Discrimination in law courts, by the police, and by other public servants.

Rank 6. Discrimination in economic activities and in access to public relief and other welfare facilities.

According to Myrdal's theory, the higher in rank the behavior, the more resistant the white population will be to granting equality in that field. Myrdal also stated that the Negro's own rank order is in inverse relation to that of the white man. The higher rank the discrimination, the less interested he is in breaking it down. By and large, Negroes concentrated their first efforts against discrimination in the ranks of least sensitivity, as Myrdal advised they should. The high resistance to school desegregation, in both North and South, as compared to the relatively low resistance to integrating Negroes into factory work shows how accurate this theory is.

It is hoped that from this chapter the reader will have acquired some idea of how a sociologist goes about his work. The chapter also illustrates the way in which sociological theory is refined bit by bit, each researcher adding his small share, until a theory is either proved or discarded as useless. The next chapter will describe some of the research which has been useful in building sociological theory.

---

[6] A summary of the research done with Bogardus' social distance scale and variations of it can be found in George E. Simpson and J. Milton Yinger, *Racial and Cultural Minorities* (New York: Harper & Row, Publishers, 1965), pp. 112–17.

[7] With the assistance of Richard Sterner and Arnold M. Rose (New York: Harper & Row, Publishers, 1st ed. 1944), pp. 60–67 of 1962 ed.

Significant Research in Sociology: Past and Present

chapter four

THE FIRST EMPIRICAL RESEARCH

In France in 1897, Emile Durkheim published a book called *Suicide*, the first piece of empirical sociological research. There had been careful compilations of fact before this and much theorizing without empirical support. In *Suicide* for the first time a major sociological theory was tested with carefully collected statistical data.

Durkheim could not find consistent associations between suicide and such factors as age, nationality, marital status, rural-urban residence, and education. He did find suicide associated with certain kinds of relationships between the individual and his society. He concluded that suicides could be classified and explained in three ways:

1. *Altruistic suicide:* The sacrifice of one's life for others, as when a soldier, for the good of his platoon, undertakes a mission from which he knows he will not escape. In this kind of suicide the individual identifies himself so closely with other members of the group that the survival of the group becomes for him the same as his own survival.
2. *Egoistic suicide:* Suicide committed by individuals who are detached from the group—the mentally ill, for example.
3. *Anomic suicide:* Suicide resulting from sudden disorganization of a society because of large-scale catastrophes or rapid social change.

The concept *anomie*, derived from the study of anomic suicide, has become one of the basic concepts of sociology because it describes the breaking of the bond which holds individuals to their groups. Durkheim's study was the first empirical demonstration of the fact that an individual cannot survive apart from a group and of some of the complicated relationships between an individual and the society to which he belongs.

The first major piece of empirical research accomplished in the United States was *The Polish Peasant in Europe and America* by William I. Thomas and Florian Znaniecki, published in 1919–21. At this period in American history, there was considerable study of the problems of immigrants, but it was limited largely to their economic and housing conditions. Thomas and Znaniecki were interested in how people raised in small, cohesive, rural villages adjusted their behavior when transplanted to large cities in an industrialized society. They followed the life stories of a number of immigrants from Poland by analyzing the contents of letters sent between the immigrants and their friends and relatives in Poland. They demonstrated that an individual tries to maintain a consistent pattern of social behavior, even when the social situation in which he lives changes drastically. The results, of course, are often mental illness, disorganization, and criminal behavior, because his internalized expectations of the society are unrealistic.

THE CHICAGO SOCIOLOGISTS STUDY THEIR CITY

At the University of Chicago, under the influence of Robert E. Park (1864–1944), sociologists in the 1920's and the 1930's began to do research on urban problems. After World War I, Chicago was a fast growing city, spreading over the surrounding, seemingly endless prairies. New neighborhoods sprang up. The inhabitants were divided into many racial and nationality groups, some of them newly arrived from Europe, some of them migrants from America's rural areas. Change was rapid; heterogeneity great; the political structure inadequate to deal with either. The Chicago sociologists, stimulated by Park's sensitivity to urban life (he had started his career as a journalist), saw the city as a great social laboratory spread before them, and as such they used it.

The Chicago studies—there were nineteen of them published between 1923 and 1933—are colorful and interesting. Louis Wirth's *The Ghetto* (1925) is a study of the effects of social isolation on a minority group. It is still a standard work. The first intimate study of a juvenile gang was Frederick Thrasher's *The Gang* (1927). No better study on the subject has yet been done. The heterogeneity of a big city was analyzed in Harvey Zorbaugh's *The Gold Coast and the Slum* (1929). The first attempts to map the geographic incidence of social problems was done in a book called *Delinquency Areas* (1929).[1] Taken together the Chicago studies form a solid theoretical and empirical foundation for urban sociology, and they are still important.

SOCIOLOGISTS REFINE THEIR PREDICTIVE TECHNIQUES

If prediction is the aim of science, it is not surprising that prediction studies have been a major concern of sociologists. When the Social Science Research Council published a comprehensive evaluation of prediction studies in 1941,[2] a study by E. W. Burgess and Leonard S. Cottrell, *Predicting Success or Failure in Marriage* (1939), was rated highly for its ability to predict accurately. Burgess and Cottrell used a questionnaire to discover the degree of happiness of their subjects and then tested the respondent's answers for accuracy and truthfulness in a variety of ways. They were then able to pick out those items on the questionnaire which predicted either success or failure in achieving happiness in marriage. The items which predicted well became the basis for a standardized test. Length of courtship, age at marriage, happiness of parents, degree of participation in church and other group activities, and attitudes toward sex were some of the factors predictive of marital happiness. It should be emphasized, however, that single items from the test do not have predictive value.

It is hard to overemphasize the importance of this pioneering study. The development of highly predictive tests has had much practical value. Marital adjustment tests are used by marriage counselors, social workers, ministers, and others as a basis for advising their clients and as an aid in diagnosing the cause of marital difficulties. The predictive technique Burgess and Cottrell invented has been refined and applied to other fields. A test was developed for the army in World War II to screen out potential psychoneurotics. There are tests which predict success or failure on parole. Others indicate potential success in certain jobs.

---

[1] Clifford Shaw *et al.*

[2] Paul Horst (ed.), *The Prediction of Personal Adjustment* (New York: The Social Science Research Council, 1941).

Delinquent or psychoneurotic behavior among children can also be predicted.

SOCIAL CHANGE AND PREDICTION

If one understands why social change occurs, one should be able to predict its results. Sociologists during the 1930's studied social trends for exactly this reason. Because they concentrated their attention mainly on economic factors, social trend research failed to predict accurately when other factors were important. It was impossible also to take into account the effects of major and unanticipated social events like World War II. Demographers, for example, usually assume that birth and death rates will vary to some extent, but they were unable to predict either the great baby boom of war and postwar days or the lowering of the death rate among the elderly due to new medical discoveries. As a consequence, all the population projections made before 1940 were much too low.

Several modern social trend studies have, however, been able to predict accurately, mainly because they took a large number of factors into account. One of these is Arnold Rose's *The Negro's Morale* (1949). Starting with slavery days, he analyzed the factors which created solidarity among the Negroes: increased literacy; the work of the Negro press in maintaining communication throughout the Negro community; devoted and effective leadership organized into protest organizations with specific and realizable aims; the success of the segregated Negro church in producing an in-group feeling; heavy migration of Negroes to the North; changes in the economic and social structure of the South, and changes in the attitudes of the white population, both North and South. He noted the ways in which increasing in-group feeling enabled the Negroes to mount an effective protest against discrimination. In 1949 he predicted approximately when and how the Negro protest would break out. The sit-ins, boycotts, and riots with which Negroes have attempted to gain their civil rights, starting in 1961, generally fulfilled his predictions.

The method of predicting used in *The Negro's Morale* was formulated by Gunnar Myrdal in *An American Dilemma* (1944). Myrdal is an economist, and his technique for predicting social changes is borrowed from economics. He calls his theoretical model the *principle of cumulative causation*. He assumes that all the factors relevant to any social change are connected in a spiral, which is moving either up or down. Any change in any of the factors will affect all the other factors and move them in the same direction as the original change was moving. For example, an increase in the educational attainments of Negroes will increase their ability to get well-paying jobs which in turn will enable them to buy better housing. Conversely, an increase in unemployment will decrease their ability to buy better housing and, because better schools are in good neighborhoods, will also decrease the possibility of getting an adequate education. This model for analyzing social change can also serve as a guide to governmental action. If Negroes are suffering from greater than average unemployment because of discrimination or low educational attainments or both, a law to prevent job discrimination and policies to increase educational opportunities will decrease unemployment. This will start the spiral of connected factors moving upwards, and it will continue under its own momentum.

COMMUNITY STUDIES

Although a society does not have to have a geographic base to be a society, some societies, like the United States, do have one. When they do, they are called *communities*. Sociological interest in studying communities goes back at least as far as the publication of W. E. B. Du Bois' study *The Philadelphia Negro* in 1899. In 1929 Robert and Helen Lynd made sociological history by publishing their famous study of Muncie, Indiana, called *Middletown*. The Lynds were trying to study the community as a whole. They went to live in Muncie and interviewed the people they met and lived with, in the same manner as anthropologists live with and interview the groups they study.

The Lynds found the Middletown economy dominated by one industry. The class structure of the community was rigid, and there was a lack of communication among groups. Participation in community affairs was confined to a few people. Middletown citizens were portrayed as unhappy and sullen.[3] Eight years later, a second volume, *Middletown in Transition,* examined the social changes the Great Depression had caused in Muncie. Economic

---

[3] The citizens of Middletown were quite unhappy when the Lynds exposed the details of their community life to a national audience. John Marquand took a more lighthearted view of the observing sociologist in his satiric and very funny novel, *Point of No Return,* about the invasion of a New England town by a group of sociologists intent on studying the inhabitants. There are no reports on how the sociologists felt about being analyzed by Marquand.

and political power was more dispersed throughout the community; there was great participation of all groups; and the citizens were much more aware of and affected by trends in the national economy.

Somewhat later (1941), W. Lloyd Warner and his associates, also using anthropological techniques, studied a New England town they called Yankee City. The results of this study were published in five volumes, each on a specialized subject. Taken together they describe the entire community. The Yankee City studies aroused controversy about the class structure of American society, which has not simmered down yet. Warner said that Yankee City residents regarded themselves and others as belonging to six different classes: lower-lower; upper-lower; lower-middle; upper-middle; lower-upper; and upper-upper. He implied that the total American class structure was similarly divided. Critics of Warner say that his classification cannot be applied in large metropolitan areas or the nation as a whole, because people do not know each other well enough to make a judgment about the class everybody belongs to. The critics seek objective criteria of class, like income or occupation. As a rule, sociologists today avoid the problem. They study differences in occupation, income, education, prestige, and status, but avoid defining classes as such.

Equally controversial was Warner's declaration (made before the publication of the Yankee City books) that Negroes constituted a caste in American society. It shocked Americans to think that other Americans were relegated to a separate category from which they were prevented from moving by law and custom. John Dollard, in his book *Caste and Class in a Southern Town* (1937), studied the extent to which segregation created a society in which people's occupations, behavior, and attitudes were fixed by their caste positions. Dollard's findings supported Warner's caste theory as did Hylan Lewis' study of the Negro section of a Southern town (*Blackways of Kent*, 1955). St. Clair Drake and Horace Cayton studied a Northern Negro community (in Chicago) and found such extreme discrimination there that the community was unable to function (*Black Metropolis*, 1945).

Both the Middletown studies and the Yankee City series were landmarks in sociology, but in dealing with the community as a whole they failed to do justice to the complexity of a modern city. They also neglected the ways in which even small towns are affected by national political policies or the condition of the national economy. James West published a study of a small, isolated Missouri town (*Plainville, U.S.A.*) in 1946. When Art Gallaher, Jr., studied the same town (*Plainville, Fifteen Years Later*, 1961), he found that economic changes in the United States had completely destroyed the isolation of the town and had changed most of the attitudes West had regarded as characteristic of the residents.

In the interest of greater completeness, later community studies have concentrated on only one aspect of a community. In *Elmtown's Youth* (1949), for example, A. B. Hollingshead studied only the youth of his community. He found that economic and social differences among the young people set them apart in their interests and aspirations, even in early adolescence.

Because large numbers of Americans now live in suburbs, studies of suburban life have been of recent interest. William M. Dobriner, in *The Suburban Community* (1958), puts to rest some of the stereotypes about suburban life. There are many kinds of suburbs inhabited by people who shortly before lived in cities. Suburban life is, therefore, not all of a piece, nor does it differ much from city life. Robert C. Wood (*Suburbia, Its People and Their Politics*, 1963) supports Dobriner's findings by examining the ways in which people express their needs and interests through a variety of political activities.

In view of this long sociological interest in community studies, it is somewhat disconcerting for a sociologist to realize that one of the best community studies of recent years has been done by a political scientist.[4] It does point up how the social sciences overlap in their interests, their conceptual schemes, and their methodology. Robert A. Dahl's book *Who Governs? Democracy and Power in an American City* (1961), a beautifully executed and highly informative piece of research, illustrates the more recent, segmentalized approach to the study of the community. Dahl is interested in only one aspect of community life—its politics—and in only one aspect of politics—who has power in a middle-sized New England city (New Haven, Connecticut) and how it is acquired and used.[5] He feels that political *power* (the ability to impose one's will on others) is widely dispersed in American communities and differentially used.

By analyzing the political history of New Haven from colonial days until 1960, Dahl is able to show that political power has shifted from the hands of an elite social group to those of professional politicians, representative of and responsive to the demands

---

[4] History repeats itself. The very earliest community studies in the United States were made by a group of political scientists at Johns Hopkins University in the 1880's.

[5] It is hoped that those who believe politics is a mystery beyond the control of the average citizen will read Dahl's fine book.

of the average citizen. In addition, he uses case studies to illustrate how and when the average citizen exerts his normally latent political power.

Dahl's theories about political behavior are in contrast to those expressed by C. Wright Mills, a sociologist, in a well-known book *The Power Elite* (1956). Mills believed that the well-to-do were also the economically and politically powerful. His work has been criticized because he did not demonstrate that having great wealth is the same as exerting great economic power. Economic power belongs to the managers of industry, but in the United States they are not the same group as the wealthy, although these groups may overlap. The owners and managers of industry are often in competition with each other, and they may have regional interests. Moreover, Mills did not demonstrate that the economically powerful controlled the political system. The President of the United States has enormous political power, but he may be a man of modest means, like Truman; a career officer, like Eisenhower; or an heir to great wealth with comparatively little economic power, like Kennedy. Members of Congress exhibit the same range of economic and social status.

Floyd Hunter, in his study of Atlanta, Georgia, *Community Power Structure* (1953), agrees to some extent with Mills. He stated that a small, economically and socially powerful group exerted great political influence in the local community.

Dahl's research was undertaken, in part, to disprove the Hunter-Mills thesis. His findings, buttressed by impressive empirical and documentary evidence, do call both Hunter's and Mills' theories into question. Whether Dahl's analysis can be applied to a large Southern city like Atlanta or to the United States as a whole is a question that waits upon further research.

DEVIANT BEHAVIOR

Sociologists have done many studies on deviant behavior—alcoholism, narcotic addiction, gambling, illegitimacy, prostitution, adult crime, and juvenile delinquency. Deviant behavior is one type of social problem. The term "deviant" assumes that most people in the society disapprove of and do not engage in this kind of behavior. If this were true, it would simplify life for sociologists. Although most people will verbally disapprove of what is classified as deviant behavior, most people engage in some kinds of deviant behavior some of the time. Disapproval really falls on those who get caught. Furthermore, all groups in a society are not agreed on what deviant behavior is. For sociologists studying deviant behavior, there is another set of tension-producing circumstances: What they recommend to cure deviant behavior, on the basis of the very best scientific evidence they can muster, is frequently unacceptable to the society. This makes sociologists very vulnerable to the suggestion that they should stop studying deviant behavior and instead find out how to get a society to change its values.

For example, those groups in the United States who habitually consume alcohol during meals and give their children liquor at an early age are the groups which do *not* produce alcoholics. Research seems to show that the habitual but restrained use of alcohol is a safeguard against alcoholism.[6] The United States is the only modern country with a high rate of drug addiction. Other countries give addicts what drugs they need under medical supervision, thus taking the profit out of the illicit drug trade and preventing addicts from engaging in crime to get the money they need to pay for drugs. Americans are unwilling to follow the advice of sociologists in either of these two situations.

Edwin H. Sutherland is responsible for two significant pieces of research in criminology. They are significant because they introduced new ideas and stimulated a great deal of subsequent research along the same lines. The first was *The Professional Thief* (1937), which pointed out that the most successful criminals were professionals, who entered into and learned their occupations in exactly the way a doctor, judge, or carpenter learns his. *White-Collar Crime* (1949) documented the fact that many crimes, costly to the society, were committed by otherwise respectable citizens and corporations. These two studies established the idea that ordinary people engage in deviant behavior. If society offers the opportunity, people learn deviant behavior in the same way they learn acceptable ways of behaving.

Recent studies of juvenile delinquency have sought to find out what it is either in the society or in the training of children that makes them susceptible to learning deviant behavior. An excellent study of this kind is Clark Vincent's *Unmarried Mothers* (1961). No single set of circumstances is responsible for illicit sexual activities, but Vincent does succeed in isolating some of

---

[6] For a comprehensive survey of research on alcoholism, see David J. Pittman and Charles R. Snyder, *Society, Culture and Drinking Patterns* (New York: John Wiley & Sons, Inc., 1962).

the factors which prevent young girls from internalizing traditional sex values.

A similar and very influential study is Albert Cohen's *Delinquent Boys, the Culture of the Gang* (1955). Gang behavior is frequently characteristic of lower-class males. They enter delinquent gangs in the same way and for the same reasons that middle-class boys enter Boy Scout troops. They evidently get the same kinds of personal satisfaction in the gang as other boys get from scout troops. The culture (meanings and values) of the gang is, however, mischievous and anti-social. The gang members are socialized into this deviant culture. If the culture of the family and school have been firmly internalized, socialization into the gang is prevented. Among lower classes, there is either inadequate family socialization or its culture is close to gang culture. There is a high correlation between gang membership and school failure. Since boys enter school many years before they typically enter a gang, we can conclude that the school has not been able to socialize these boys either.

Most of sociology consists of reports and analyses of research studies. What has been presented in this chapter is an arbitrary sampling of the most significant studies conducted by sociologists. It should be noted that good research is not necessarily recent research and that some of the earliest studies are as important today as when they were done. On the other hand some research—like Sutherland's or Myrdal's—introduces new ideas, starts research in new directions, and outmodes older work.

The next chapter will present the most significant findings of sociology. Sometimes it will be evident to the reader that the supporting research has been reported in this or earlier sections. If not, the reader should assume that there is research which documents or supports the statements.

The Fundamental Insights of Sociology   chapter five

At the end of the first chapter, the reader was introduced to the idea of the "sociological perspective"—the special point of view of sociologists. Each succeeding chapter has attempted to give definition and specificity to the sociological perspective.

The first part of Chapter 2 pointed out the importance of the cosmopolitanism of sociology, both in the past and today, for establishing the possibility of universal generalizations. The second part of Chapter 2 traced the growth of sophisticated theory, adequate to explain the complexity of social reality. In Chapter 3 we explored the ways sociologists have adapted scientific methodology to the study of social data and looked into some of the ingenious ways sociologists have solved their research problems. Chapter 4 examined many of the research accomplishments of sociology to display both the range of sociological interests and the conclusions yielded by studies.

Chapter 5 contains those insights (expressed sometimes as definitions and assumptions, other times as generalizations, concepts, or theories) sociologists regard as the core of their perspective. These insights, taken together, enable sociologists to put order into observed human behavior in such a fashion that they can understand how it is caused.

The term "perspective" is relevant in another way. Sociological theory has been constructed by viewing social data from a number of viewpoints. The concept of role, for example, has one dimension when viewed as individual behavior; another when seen as a constituent of culture; and a third when described as a part of social structure. The family can be viewed as the prototype of a primary

43

group, as a socializing agency, or as an institution. In this chapter, then, society will be analyzed from a series of viewpoints, focusing successively on the individual, the group, culture, and social process, while at the same time keeping entirely within the specialized approach of sociology.

THE INDIVIDUAL AND THE GROUP

The individual and the group are the two poles about which sociological theory revolves. Everybody is born into an on-going group. This is likely to be a family. The group precedes the individual, and the social traits of the individual are inculcated by the group; the individual takes over and internalizes the meanings and values of the group and thus becomes both a member of the group and a socialized individual. The process by which this is accomplished is called socialization and occurs in the following manner:

SOCIALIZATION

In the family parents and siblings expect certain things of the young child. When the child does something the parents consider undesirable, they say, "No, no," and accompany these words with a frown or by nodding their head from side to side, or even by slapping the child's hands. The child thus learns what the parents expect (what they mean and what they value) when they use the words, "No, no," or any of the usual accompanying gestures.

At some point, the child can and does say to himself, "Johnny, no, no," and responds to the expectations he himself has raised by refraining from doing something he has learned to expect will bring negative reactions. The child has put himself into his parent's place. He has become an object to himself just as he has been an object to his parents. He begins to see himself as others see him, to evaluate his behavior and appearance as he thinks others are evaluating them, and to have a sense of shame or pride about the evaluations he thinks others make of him. He acquires an image of himself reflected by the attitudes of others just as if he saw himself in a looking-glass. His social self has emerged. He is beginning to be socialized. The social self is the end product of the process of socialization.

The social self emerges somewhere around the age of two. Until that time the expectations directed toward a child are those suitable to his age. But at two a child has been able to internalize only a small part of the society to which he belongs. He is not a full-fledged member of his own family. He will not yet have had contacts with his neighborhood or with the school which he will surely have later. As he learns what his family expects of him at later ages and what kinds of behavior his neighbors and his teachers and his peers expect, he will become more socialized. He internalizes a greater variety of expectations coming to him from more and different people. During the whole of life, whenever one enters a new group and internalizes the expectations of the other group members, socialization takes place.

Unsocialized individuals are not fully human. Babies kept in hospitals or orphanages for the first few months of their lives fail to develop either physically or mentally. When nurses are told to pick up the babies regularly and fondle and caress them as a mother does, the children begin to develop normally. At this age expectations consist of gestures and meaningless verbalizations, but some kind of communication, even though it is simple, is evidently essential for human development. Children whose parents direct contradictory expectations toward them, being severe today and permissive tomorrow, fail to become adequately socialized because they never can learn what is expected of them. Their self-image is distorted as if there were defects in the looking-glass in which they see themselves. Some mentally ill people can be described as inadequately socialized in this same way.

Individuals can also become desocialized. The Communist technique of brain-washing is a technique for desocialization. Although the precipitating causes of mental illness are manifold, many of the mentally ill can be described as desocialized.[1] Prisoners returning to society and those confined to hospitals for a long period must be resocialized to some extent. This is why criminologists and psychiatrists try to keep people out of institutions in the first place and recommend half-way houses for returnees in which resocialization into the larger society can take place.

Roles. Expectations, important components of socialization, can be further analyzed from the point of view of individual behavior. The expectations directed toward an individual during socialization are not random and unorganized. Group members have in their minds certain *sets of organized meanings and values called roles.* It is these roles they direct toward others, and it is roles, rather than separate expectations, that are internalized. Once a role is internalized an individual can direct his behavior in accordance with it. For example, "Wash your hands," "Sit up straight," "Don't hit your sister" are a few of the enormous number

---

[1] When the society is so disorganized that a large number of individuals become desocialized, *anomie* is said to be present. See pp. 33–34.

of expectations that make up the role of the "well-behaved middle-class boy." They imply certain values. Expectations can be conveyed positively—by approval and rewards—as well as negatively, and they are as often conveyed subtly as directly.

As a result of the constant flow of expectations of any group, the member has a general idea of how he is expected to behave. He knows what his roles are. The role of mother in American suburban culture includes preparing meals for her children, taking them to the dentist, reading to them, supervising their TV programs, and belonging to the PTA. In some cultures the role of mother includes very little more than bearing children and taking minimal care of them for two or three years. Strictly speaking, a role does not refer to acted-out behavior but to ideas in the mind. It is better to think of roles in this way because, when the individual acts, his actions reflect a number of roles in his mind which he has integrated[2] in some way.

One does not act out pure roles. For example, when a mother gets up at two in the morning to give her baby a bottle, she may be acting out both the general role of "mother" and the more specific role of "responsible mother." She may also be manifesting the idea that the two o'clock feeding is part of the wife's job, her role, rather than that of the husband's. While the baby is nursing, the mother may be reading a book in preparation for a sociology examination the following week in pursuance of her role as student, or career woman, or that of the "wife who keeps up her intellectual interests."

Roles sometimes conflict. The contents of the role of mother and that of career woman may conflict, but if the individual is to act at all she must make some integration of the ideas that comprise these two roles. An action may reflect part of each role, or one role may not be acted out at any one moment. If one acts out one of a conflicting pair of roles at one point in time and the other role at some other time, one's actions become inconsistent. Studies have been made of the *role conflict* a child undergoes when the demands of home and school are not the same as those of his peer group. A worker who becomes a foreman can be torn between his loyalty to the company and his identification with the workers.

Primary Groups

A different kind of analysis can emerge when attention is shifted from the individual to the group. Sociologists are not only interested in what goes on *inside* the family. They also ask whether the family is a group specialized for accomplishing socialization

---

[2] It is the *I*, of course, that does the integrating. See p. 19.

and whether similar groups exist. They find that groups can be *differentiated by their structure.* By the structure of a group, sociologists mean the usual and typical kinds of relationships that take place among group members. The family is a *primary group* because it is the first group human beings participate in and because it is the group in which people learn the primary skills of interaction and communication (socialization). Some local neighborhoods, friendship groups, and some work groups also have the structure of a primary group. In small tribes or in small villages, the whole society may be one big primary group, although this was much more common in the past than today.

Common sense tells us that membership in a primary group is important to small children, but sociologists find that it is also important for adults. The importance of primary-group relationships to adults was discovered accidentally. Because there were too few psychiatrists in mental institutions to give all the patients the attention they needed, psychiatrists began to treat patients in groups. The improvement in the patients was little short of miraculous, and the doctors began to ask why. Inadvertently, they had established primary groups, and the patients were communicating and interacting with each other. Primary-group therapy is now well understood and has been extended from mental institutions to general hospitals to aid in faster recovery of patients. In advanced prisons, group therapy is used to rehabilitate prisoners. The success of Alcoholics Anonymous seems to depend on the primary-group contacts achieved within it. The Black Muslim movement, a small and aggressive Negro protest group, has had remarkable success in curing drug addiction among its members. This, too, seems to be the result of primary-group relationships.

The usefulness of establishing primary groups to handle social problems has led to new theoretical explanations of deviant groups. Chief among these are the explanations of delinquent gangs as primary groups in which children are socialized when the home or school has failed in socialization.[3]

Secondary Groups

Any group not a primary group is called a *secondary group.* Participation in secondary groups is impersonal, segmental (one does not express all his personality), and can be of short duration. Typically, one belongs to many secondary groups in

---

[3] An excellent summary of primary-group research centering around children's problems is contained in the first few chapters of Arno Jewett, Joseph Merand, and Doris V. Gunerson (eds.), *Improving English Skills of Culturally Different Youth in Large Cities* (Washington, D.C.: U.S. Department of Health, Education, and Welfare, 1964).

a modern, pluralistic society. All secondary groups are not structured alike. A widespread kind of secondary group in our society is the *bureaucracy*.

A bureaucracy is a hierarchical form of social organization, best represented by the diagram of a triangle with a few people at the top and many below. A bureaucracy is an orderly or rational kind of organization based on written rules. It is assumed that the few people at the top have most of the power, but also that they have it because they meet reasonable and specified requirements. The ways in which one moves from the bottom of the pyramid to the top are also clearly specified, as are the relationships among all the members of a bureaucracy. Bureaucracies are slow to change and have no mechanism for adaptation to individual needs. If it is not written down in the rules, it does not exist. The army is a good example of a bureaucracy. So are American governments, with their written constitutions. Industry, schools, unions, even large religious denominations, are organized hierarchically.

Another common kind of secondary group is the *voluntary association*. When people have some common interest or common problem, they frequently band together to pursue their interests or to solve the problem. The National Bridge Association, The American Medical Association, The Audubon Society, the Red Cross, the Boy Scouts, sororities and fraternities, political clubs, businessmen's and taxpayers' associations, unions, and farm organizations are examples of voluntary associations.

Voluntary associations try to keep their members informed on what is going on within their area of interest. When the members think legislation should be passed, they frequently act as pressure groups, as the National Education Association does, for example, on matters of education. Because voluntary associations are widespread over the country, their information-spreading and lobbying activities distribute political power and enable the individual citizen to exert a measure of direct control over his affairs.

The Relationships Between Primary and Secondary Groups

Some people show great ability to understand bureaucratic structures and can fulfill their needs and rise rapidly in them. Most people, however, find their desires and needs inadequately fulfilled in bureaucracies. Particularly common is the feeling of being manipulated and at the mercy of impersonal forces, even though the people at the top of the bureaucracy may have been elected to their positions by popular vote and can be removed by proper procedures. As a result, there frequently grows up within the formal structure of the bureaucratic organization an informal structure which provides ways of circumventing the rules, of expediting services, of obtaining special privileges, of gaining access to information on the lower levels that properly should be confined to higher levels so that future events may be anticipated, and, in general, of controlling one's own destiny.

The informal structures that grow up inside bureaucracies are primary groups. Since almost everybody has had experience living in the family, it is not surprising that they enter into the same kind of relationships outside the family whenever they can. The impersonal production line of the factory is controlled by primary groups of workers who mutually agree to restrict their output. Girls in mechanized offices form intimate cliques. High school students seek prestige among their peers by assuming the peer group's values, rather than satisfying the school bureaucracy's ends by getting good grades. Informal political structures—ward machines—arise to give people information about and access to the political bureaucracy.

Many directors of bureaucracies, having become aware of how important primary group contacts are to people, deliberately stimulate the formation of primary groups. Factory managers who do this are often rewarded by an increase in production and a decrease in absenteeism and grievances. To lessen the impact of bureaucracy, large universities sometimes provide family-type residences for their students and often divide entering students into small groups which stay together during the period of orientation.

When voluntary associations are successful and become nation wide in membership, they frequently turn into bureaucracies. Even so, they usually have local chapters, some of which are primary groups. Some individuals turn voluntary associations into primary groups for themselves by devoting their whole lives to the group. For a great many people voluntary associations are something in between a primary and a secondary group. Contacts are intimate, although less so than in the family, and the individual often finds meaningful goals for himself in the work of the group. This is one aspect of socialization. The kindergarten class is a good example of a group which is less primary than the family, but does have some of the characteristics of a primary group.

COMMUNICATION

There are still further ways a sociologist can look at social phenomena. During the process of socialization, people are communicating with one another. Starting from this observation, sociologists have discovered that groups can be divided into those in which the members communicate with each other and those in which they do not. There are relatively few of the latter and almost all human groupings fall into the first category. Sociologists summarize these observations by saying that *social life is the result of communication and interaction.* A *society* or *integrated group* is any group of people interacting and communicating among themselves. Most sociologists do not think of a society solely as a large city or nation. A family is a society, so is a class of students, the National Educational Association, a hospital ward, or a boy's gang. On the basis of size, permanency, and other characteristics, sociologists distinguish groupings of people by the terms "group," "organization," and "institution." Each of these types, however, is a society or communicating group.

A family is a society because the family members talk to each other and mutually adjust their behavior (interact). When junior and sister and father all want the car at the same time, they must make demands, justify their demands, try to see the others' points of view, and come to some decision. They do not have to agree. They may get angry. They may hate each other, but they do interact and communicate with each other.

Communication among members of the National Educational Association is not necessarily face to face and intimate, but it exists. To become a member one has to send in dues. In return one receives the literature of the group and is notified of policies and meetings one may attend and participate in. The degree of participation among the members may vary enormously. Some people pay dues and do nothing else for the group, while others may devote most of their lives to furthering the aims of the group. In both cases there is some communication with other members of the group.

In contrast, window-shoppers do not communicate with each other at all, either by word or gesture. People may bump into one another without either getting angry or apologizing. If an accident should occur on the street and the passers-by stop to help, a society might develop. A person trained in first aid might assume charge and direct others. There might be argument and discussion as to the best thing to do. Communication and interaction would occur. Such a society is, of course, ephemeral and is of less interest to sociologists than a universal and basic group like the family. The formation of a society out of a casual crowd does illustrate that the mere grouping together or aggregating of people does not produce a society. Communication must be present.

Crowds, Audiences, and Publics

When communication does not occur among group members, we speak of *nonintegrated* groups, and some of these are becoming increasingly important in modern society. A group of window-shoppers is called a *casual crowd*. A group of people wildly excited but not communicating with each other—as the spectators at a football match or people fleeing in panic from a theater fire—is called an *expressive crowd*. If someone can make himself heard in a panicked crowd and establish communication between himself and the crowd members, he can turn an expressive crowd into a society, which can take deliberate and sensible common action.

A third kind of crowd is the *acting crowd*—a lynch mob or a group of rioters. Once a crowd begins to form, communication ceases. Members of the crowd respond to the physical nearness of others, the commonly generated excitement, meaningless shouts and noises. Again, if somebody can re-establish communication before the crowd begins to act, a society emerges, and mob action never takes place. Police are trained in methods of turning a crowd into a society.

The people listening to a TV program also are not a society. They are responding individually to a common stimulus—the program. If they do not ever communicate with each other, they are called an *audience*. If the program is, let us say, a broadcast of a national political convention and people discuss it with their friends and acquaintances next day or write letters to the newspapers about what transpired, we call the group a *public*. A public is a large, informal discussion group and provides indirect communication among its members, usually through the mass media. A public is thus in some respects like an integrated group, although it resembles nonintegrated groups as well.

Sociologists do not make these distinctions on the basis of whether or not there is communication among group members because of a desire for hair-splitting precision. The absence of communication among the members of a group has severe and usually undesirable consequences. Those that follow the formation of an expressive or acting crowd are obvious. The effect of having many audiences in a society is not so clear.

If people do not communicate with each other but respond only to an outside stimulus, they lose the ability to communicate. For the individual this may mean mental illness just as if he were locked up away from people. Democracy cannot exist in a nation in which people engage largely or entirely in audience behavior instead of communicating with one another, either directly or indirectly.

Mass Society

George Orwell's novel *1984* portrays a *mass* society, one in which the members are completely manipulated through propaganda directed to audiences through the mass media. Nazi Germany was a mass society; many Communist countries are almost mass societies. Sociologists regard anything that breaks down communication as dangerous to democracy, and this is why they are concerned about the extent to which people watch TV or are spectators at sports rather than active participants in groups.

In the past year (1964) the newspapers have reported several occasions in which bystanders refused to go to the aid of women being attacked. In one case people were watching through their windows and had access to telephones, but, out of thirty-five spectators, only one called the police and then not until almost an hour had passed. In another case, the attack took place in a crowded office building, and the woman called repeatedly for help. These examples of audience rather than participant or interacting behavior worry sociologists more than crime or changes in values.

In a large, heterogeneous society such as most modern societies are, communication throughout the whole society is difficult to maintain. The mass media—radio, newspapers, magazines, and TV—can spread common information over a wide area. The transformation of this information into common values and meanings depends on the way groups are structured and the extent to which people participate in them.

The establishment of many publics, largely by permitting free communication, is one way of combatting audience behavior. Another is the proliferation of voluntary associations which, by informing and orienting their members in a mass society, enable them to control their destinies by rational collective action.

Since communication seems to be a key or distinguishing characteristic of many groups, sociologists have tried to analyze and find out more about it. While some communication takes place by signs and gestures, it is immediately apparent that almost all human communication is verbal and proceeds from *mind* to *mind*. This has prompted sociologists to say that society exists in the minds of its members. Modern sociology is based firmly on the assumption that a society needs neither a geographic base nor artifacts (material things) to exist but consists of the *sum* of the *ideas* held by all the individuals who make up a group.

This is a very difficult thing to comprehend, and yet it is one of the most essential elements of the sociological perspective. It is difficult to think of the United States without thinking of its territory spreading from ocean to ocean, its farms and cities, its schools and factories, its automobiles and airplanes. If, however, Americans suddenly disappeared, leaving intact all their material possessions, there would be no society. Conversely, if a large group of Americans were stranded in a remote place, there is no doubt that, within the physical possibilities available, they would recreate a society organized around prevailing American values.[4]

When a teacher thinks of "my class," she probably thinks of it within a specific classroom having certain books, maps, and other artifacts at its disposal. But the class exists only when the members and the teachers are communicating with each other. When class is dismissed the group ceases to exist until all are assembled again. Each member carries part of the class in his mind, and it takes all the minds together to make the class.

Not only do sociologists find it necessary to think of society as existing in the minds of its members in order to get a clear picture of what society is, but there are also practical reasons for maintaining this point of view. For example, statistical analysis shows that juvenile delinquency, alcoholism, family disorganization, and other unpleasant phenomena occur more frequently in blighted and run-down neighborhoods of the city than they do in better-kept residential areas. With the best intentions in the world, Americans jumped to the conclusion that, if the facilities of blighted areas were improved or if the residents were moved to other neighborhoods, these social problems would disappear. Despite the expenditure of billions of dollars on low-cost housing and urban renewal, neither of these solutions has worked. Disorganized families are just as disorganized in bright, new housing projects as they were in the slums, because they carry their society with them in their minds.

When urban renewal was started and the blighted areas examined one by one, so that their individual characteristics were not lost in statistical averages, it was found that many of the neighborhoods were highly organized. The residents, far from suffering from social problems, were happy and able to mobilize themselves to oppose destruction of their neighborhoods. Again, the significant fact was the ideas in the minds of people and not the external aspects of the neighborhoods.

---

[4]William Golding's novel, *Lord of the Flies* (London: Faber, 1954), illustrates this well. A group of English boys, stranded on an island, established exactly the kind of primitive, violent society one would expect of half-socialized young males. The English naval officer who rescued them said, "Bad show for English boys." As a fully socialized adult, he had very different ideas of what constitutes a "good society."

CULTURE

The location of society in the minds of its members does not simplify the task of sociologists. What goes on in the minds of individuals cannot be directly observed. It can only be inferred from external behavior—from the way in which an individual behaves either toward

1. objects (what their meaning is to him) or
2. other people (the nature of his interactions).

The most frequently observed external behavior is verbal—what a person says he thinks or believes or wants or dislikes or what he says to another person. On page 44 the description of what goes on in the mind of the small child during socialization is an example of this kind of analysis.

But sociologists also try to find out what is going on in the minds of all the people of a group. They are concerned about the meanings and values that are *shared* by group members. This can be stated as follows: *A culture consists of the shared meanings and values that the members of any group hold in common.* Culture is acquired through the interaction and communication that goes on among the members of a group.

A *meaning* is similar to a dictionary definition and tells people how to behave toward an object. The usual meaning of the word "chair" is "something to sit on." Of course, a chair can have many meanings. It can also be "the antique I inherited from my grandmother," "something to kick at when angry," or, to a child at play, "the engine of my train." Meanings vary from group to group. An automobile may mean convenient transportation to suburbanites, independence and prestige to teenagers. In the United States a bicycle is used for recreation, mainly by young people. In an underdeveloped country, it may mean wealth and power to the owner. In some European countries a bicycle is a means of adult transportation. The bicycle, the artifact, does not vary; the meaning of it does.

A *value* is any attitude which has some positive or negative emotion connected with it. Some values are commonly accepted by a group, but failure to conform to these values does not arouse much excitement. Although it is customary for women to wear a hat to a Protestant church service and most women do, someone otherwise properly dressed would cause little comment if she went hatless to church. Other values are strongly held, and, if they are violated, the violator may be gossiped about, ostracized, or deprived of public esteem.

Public esteem is also bestowed on individuals in order to encourage desirable behavior. Occasionally a school will award letters for scholarship as they do for excellence in athletics in an attempt to increase the public esteem awarded to bright students. This device may not always work, but it indicates that most people are aware of the social function of public esteem.

Some values the group regards as essential for its welfare. These are called *mores* and there are not many of them in a modern society. Today in the United States, our mores forbid such things as incest, cannibalism, and treason. For the most part, people do not violate the mores, and if they do the group's disapproval is immediate, spontaneous, and violent. Theoretically, the values of any group can be arranged along a continuum with those least strongly held at one end and the mores at the other.

When a country has many groups in it, each with its own set of meanings and values (as has the United States), social change is inevitable. Individuals belong to many groups and thus acquire and hold simultaneously different and sometimes conflicting values which they must somehow reconcile. The values of whole groups of people are given expression by their leaders and other spokesmen and become known and debated through the mechanism of the public. Thus, pluralistic societies have one kind of social change built into them. Only in isolation can a group maintain its culture unchanged.

The white Southerner's belief in the segregation of whites and Negroes is a strongly held value, but it is changing. Large numbers of white Southerners have gone into the racially integrated armed services, have gone North to work or to school. There they have been exposed to a different set of values about the capacities of the Negro and his place in society. Industrialization of the South has brought Northerners to live there, and they have carried their ideas into the South. Television, radio, and the mass circulation magazines have exposed Southerners to new ideas. As a result of the breakdown of Southern isolation, the old value system of the South is fast disappearing. The reader should note that this discussion of how values change answers some of the questions about consensus raised in Chapter 2, page 18.

Culture is not a miscellaneous collection of meanings and values. Meanings and values cluster together and are called roles. When we met the concept of role before, we were looking at it from the point of view of an individual. From this perspective, role was seen as a pattern of behavior directed, in the form of expectations, from one person to another and accepted as a guide to behavior.

From another perspective, a group can be thought of as a complex of roles. The family, for example, can be thought of as the combined roles of father, mother, wife, husband, parent, son, daughter, child, brother, and sister. To these we can add such roles as henpecked husband, career woman, nagging wife, philandering husband, devoted daughter, and the myriad of others one can think of.

Within any group the members evaluate group roles differently. A leader is more highly regarded than a rank-and-file member, and members must have certain qualities before they can become leaders. Mothers are evaluated differently than fathers or brothers and sisters. Each role complements all other roles so that the totality of roles in any group forms a functioning whole.[5] A school has those who learn as well as those who teach, those who supervise and direct as well as those who look after the health of the students or who clean up the building. Each of the individuals who fill these roles has some position (status) in the group relative to all other members of the group. Every role thus has a status attached to it, and some sociologists speak of status-role instead of role.

From the point of view of the group, role conflict also takes on new dimensions. Some role conflicts are solved by developing a new role which synthesizes elements of the old conflicting roles. When this happens in a major social role, the structure of the group can be changed. The changing roles of women affect the basic structure of the family and permanently alter the relationships among family members. The altering of relationships among people is what is meant by *role change*.

Sociologists have concepts other than role which can be used to analyze culture. They abstract out *systems of meanings and values* and call them *ideologies*. All the phrases that are used to justify American democracy and all the behavior Americans as citizens are expected to engage in or refrain from doing form the democratic ideology. Groups have *symbols* [6] which stand for the

---

[5] Remember that we are talking about patterns of behavior and not individuals. If a family has no mother, the father or an older sister or an outsider may play the role, or they may share it. If no one plays a major role in the group, the group is described as disorganized to at least some degree.

[6] A very easy to read and enlightening book about symbols in a mass society is Orrin E. Klapp, *Symbolic Leaders: Public Dramas and Public Men* (Chicago: Aldine Publishing Co., 1964).

meanings and values of the ideology, as the American flag stands for democracy. Part of an ideology consists of *myths* which illustrate and explain an ideology. The myth that "anybody can be President" is a shorthand way of saying that we have a free society without rigid class lines. One learns an ideology in the same way one learns a role—through internalizing the expectations directed toward one by a group. When children recite the "Pledge of Allegiance" in a classroom they are performing a *ritual* before a *symbol* of the *ideology* of American democracy. This is one way they learn the ideology. When a child who belongs to the Jehovah's Witnesses refrains from reciting the "Pledge," he experiences role conflict and is in the middle of an ideological conflict.

SOCIAL PROCESSES

A final perspective from which sociologists analyze societies focuses on the social act. Earlier in the chapter we described the simplest kind of social act, the unit of interaction, when we recounted what goes on when a parent directs expectations to a child and the child constructs a response. When one social act follows another and depends upon or proceeds from the prior act, sociologists speak of a *social process*. Interaction, either between or among individuals or between or among groups, occurs in the form of social processes. Sociologists have found that the *kinds of relationships among groups and among group members are universal and recurrent*. There are hundreds of social processes, but some are far more important than others.

Everywhere children are born into families and learn the ways of their society. They undergo *socialization*. Nations go to war with each other; children in the nursery fight; and the Democrats try to defeat the Republicans at election time. In all three cases *conflict* is occurring. Students in a class vie for grades, and businessmen try to win customers from each other. Both the students and the businessmen are engaging in *competition*.

The social process of conflict is second in importance only to socialization. Conflict is a basic social process because by engaging in conflict with each other, groups determine their relationships, one to another. A stable, organized society controls conflict. It limits it with rules of the game. Political conflict in the United States is a good example of this. It takes place by persuasion and propaganda, not by violence. The losers accept their defeat, and the winners restrain their vengeance. Collective bargaining between labor and industry is another example of limited conflict. A large amount of conflict is channeled through the courts.

After conflict has ended, new relationships may be established. The union may have gained recognition and more power in the economic system. The Republicans may have control of the political system. After race riots the Negroes' rights have frequently been recognized and guaranteed. Conflict is thus one of the major ways in which social change takes place.

Traditional societies are stratified into classes or castes, some of which have more power than others. Shifts of power occur only through conflict among the classes, as in the Cuban revolution led by Castro. In an open-class society such as ours, conflict is often replaced by competition. Individuals and groups vie with one another for identical goals. The progress of one impedes the progress of another, but there is no personal antagonism toward or, possibly even identification of, the competitors. Individuals and groups compete with each other for better education or for more money or for power and prestige. The ability to control valued items can thus move from individual to individual and from group to group without conflict.

If space permitted, it would be possible to list other important sociological insights. Those we have chosen for this chapter fit together into a systematic, integrated theory, along with the other material presented in the earlier parts of the book, to which we have sometimes referred in footnotes.

The necessity of compressing a great deal of material into a brief space has resulted in a presentation which seems more systematic than it really is. Conflicts among sociologists, ambiguities, and the problem of lack of sufficient empirical proof have not been presented. Nevertheless, the author feels that this chapter does present a comprehensive and balanced description of modern sociological theory.

Epilogue

The word root, *socius* (bond, tie, relationship), loosely translated, means "group." In English it also has the connotation of something good for the welfare of the group. We speak of social as opposed to asocial behavior. For this reason and because many sociologists study social problems, there is a widespread impression that sociologists are "do-gooders"—that their primary purpose is to do good. One sociologist has found it necessary in his introductory text to distinguish sociology from "socialism," an economic and political creed, and from "social work," a profession whose primary purpose *is* to alleviate social problems.

These misunderstandings crush sociologists who dearly wish to be recognized as scientists. It is hoped that this little book will have demonstrated that sociology is a science and a reasonably well-developed one. There is a very practical reason for recognizing that this is so. A science is value-free. Its findings can be used equally for good or evil purposes just as knowledge about the atom can be used to create bombs or to provide cheap industrial power. Sociologists are no better or worse than other men. They are of all political persuasions. They embrace as wide a range of values as any other group does. They can no more be depended upon to permit their findings to be used only for good ends than can the physicists be depended on not to provide the knowledge to make nuclear weapons.

Sociologists already control techniques that could be put to questionable uses. They know how to desocialize people (brainwashing). They know how to manipulate people through the mass media. They know how to build up or break down the morale of groups, a process that could be used by industry to destroy a union, for example, or by a corrupt national union leader to destroy an intransigent local. It is important, therefore, that the average citizen have some knowledge of the findings of sociology. He needs also to realize that it is the citizens of a democracy who must decide what values and policies should be implemented and not a group of scientists, no matter how reassuring the name of their profession is. Just as the findings of sociology can be put to evil uses, however, so can they be used to implement moral ends, as we have tried to indicate throughout this book.

Probably most of the members of any profession privately think their own profession superior to others. Somebody once called sociology, "the Queen of the Social Sciences." Although publicly sociologists repudiate this statement in the interests of harmony with their colleagues in the other sciences, privately most of us do believe that sociology *is* basic to all other social sciences. Whether it is or not, the findings of sociology should be known more widely, particularly in the secondary schools. It is hoped that the teachers who read this book will find sociology useful.

The writing of a book like this is, of course, a teaching effort. It has been both difficult and rewarding: difficult because communication is an art one never masters completely; rewarding because, as Henry Adams said, "A teacher affects eternity; he can never tell where his influence stops."

Suggested Methods for Teachers

chapter six

Raymond H. Muessig
Vincent R. Rogers

INTRODUCTION

When we traverse the gallery of history, and observe its
motley succession of fantastic paintings—when we examine in
a cursory way the successive races of mankind, all different
and constantly changing, our first impression is apt to be that
the phenomena of social life are incapable of any general
expression or scientific law, and that the attempt to found a
system of sociology is wholly chimerical. But the first herds-
men who scanned the starry heavens, and the first tillers of
the soil who essayed to discover the secrets of plant life, must
have been impressed in much the same way by the sparkling
disorder of the firmament, with its manifold meteors, as well
as by the exuberant diversity of vegetable and animal forms.
The idea of explaining sky or forest by a small number of
logically concatenated notions, under the name of astronomy
or biology, had it occurred to them, would have appeared in
their eyes the height of extravagance. And there is no less
complexity—no less irregularity and apparent caprice—in the
world of meteors and in the interior of the virgin forest, than
in the recesses of human history.[1]

In this fascinating, poetic paragraph written by Gabriel Tarde,
the French criminologist, penologist, philosopher, psychologist, and
sociologist, one gets a feeling for the difficulties and challenges of
sociology as perceived by an early pioneer. While this passage
dates back to the very late nineteenth century, it contains elements

---

[1] Gabriel Tarde, "From *Social Laws*," in Robert Bierstedt (ed.), *The Making
of Society* (New York: Modern Library, Inc., 1959), p. 316.

61

of truth and insight even today. Sociology, the compelling study of man's social behavior, still tussles with complex, elusive, constantly changing subject matter that defies test-tube precision.

Oliver Wendell Holmes once remarked that "if the whole *materia medica* as now used could be sunk to the bottom of the sea, it would be all the better for mankind—and all the worse for the fishes." Perhaps there are those outside of the discipline of sociology and a few working within this broad field who occasionally have an urge to issue a similar statement about their area. Yet the fact that the common cold, the "virus" (a word physicians at times seem to employ when they have no idea what is causing a particular illness), and countless other physical disorders continue to baffle medical doctors has not kept them from continuing their research and their endeavors to alleviate human suffering and to extend life. In the same way, there is a great deal that the sociologist does not know and cannot explain with surety, but he persists in his efforts to probe social phenomena and to help groups of people gain the knowledge about society and its functions that will enable them to identify and move closer towards elements of the good life as they perceive it.

We believe that children and youth can and should have a glimpse of social forces and processes at work in their lives and in the lives of others; that they can profit from some exposure to societal issues, problems, desires, and accomplishments; that they can grow intellectually and emotionally as a result of their contact with selected aspects of the discipline of sociology; and that they can learn and use carefully selected understandings, skills, and attitudes drawn from sociology for use in social studies curricula. To borrow the title of a book by W. Lloyd Warner,[2] we feel that our young people should examine "American life: dream and reality" as objectively and creatively as possible, in many ways and at various conceptual levels.

To date, the writers are not aware of any conclusive experimental evidence which indicates that particular aspects of sociology are uniquely suited for utilization in social studies programs at given grade levels. It appears that quite a few sociological generalizations and concepts could be presented from the primary grades through senior high school if appropriate adjustments are made in light of children's varying conceptual abilities. Our work with both children and experienced elementary school teachers has led us to conclude that sociology lends itself readily to meaningful application in the lower grades. Research indicates that many of the

[2] *American Life: Dream and Reality* (Chicago: The University of Chicago Press, 1953).

expressed interests and concerns of senior high school students are clearly sociological in nature, so sociology deserves consideration for inclusion at this level as well. At all instructional levels, elements of sociology can be tapped as teachers guide their students in the pursuit of widely accepted social studies objectives.

In this chapter we have chosen to provide methodological illustrations for five significant sociological ideas. Other over-all generalizations suggested themselves to us as we read the preceding five chapters by Mrs. Rose, so these major statements should be regarded as representative and by no means exhaustive.

1. Man Is a Social Animal Who Lives Always in Groups. He May Belong to a Variety of Groups, Each of Which Can Be Differentiated by Its Structure.

During his three-score and ten years on earth, a human being may belong to many groups. Every one of these groups is made up of individuals whose relationships to each other are patterned in various ways. Some groups have rather unique characteristics, while others possess a number of properties in common. One group is typified by direct, intimate, face-to-face associations; another is not. Groups vary in their intensity of purpose, exercise of authority, utilization of sanctions and forms of reinforcement, repetitive actions and interactions, traditions, continuity, and ability to satisfy the needs of their members. But whatever the nature of a group, its composition and functions can be investigated and analyzed. Since so much of what makes humankind human is a product of group life, we feel that an examination of man and the groups to which he belongs should have a place at all levels of instruction.

Teachers might approach this initial sociological generalization by using appropriate literary materials to help students identify a number of groups and to offer possible reasons for their existence and outcomes of their activities. With children in the primary grades, for example, the teacher could read aloud a story such as *Elephant Herd* by Miriam Schlein.[3] The story concerns the strength and security that exist as long as the elephants band together in a herd. *One* elephant would find it very difficult indeed to cope with the many dangers of life in the jungle, but *together* the herd has a reasonable chance for survival.

Children should quickly perceive the protective and educative functions of a group through an expanded discussion of *Elephant Herd* and should be able to suggest corresponding examples in human groups of different sizes and kinds.

---

[3] New York: The Junior Literary Guild and William R. Scott, Inc., 1954.

Similarly, pupils in every school grade could discover that many groups help individuals satisfy needs and achieve larger purposes which would be beyond the capacity of a single person. With children in the intermediate grades, for instance, the teacher might use material like this which deals with the dramatic accomplishment of the skilled crew of the first atomic-powered submarine, the *Nautilus*:

> Commander Anderson stepped to the mike of the ship's public address system.
> "All hands . . . this is the Captain speaking . . . In a few moments, *Nautilus* will realize a goal long a dream of mankind—the attainment by ship of the North Geographic Pole. With continued Godspeed, in less than two days we will record an even more significant historic first: the completion of a rapid transpolar voyage from the Pacific to the Atlantic Ocean.
> "The distance to the Pole is now precisely four-tenths of a mile. As we approach, let us pause in silence dedicated with our thanks for the blessings that have been ours during this remarkable voyage—our prayers for lasting world peace, and in solemn tribute to those who have preceded us, whether in victory or defeat."
>
> . . . .
>
> The distance indicator showed that the nose of the *Nautilus* was seconds away from the Pole. The captain began his countdown to the crew.
> "Stand by. 10 . . . 8 . . . 6 . . . 4 . . . 3 . . . 2 . . . 1. MARK! August 3, 1958. Time, 2315 (11:15 Eastern Daylight Savings Time). For the United States and the United States Navy, the North Pole!"
> Cheers burst out from all hands. They shook the ship, rattled plates, cups, and pans in the galley.[4]

Students will find, too, that a large number of groups perform social functions. Family and friendship groups, clubs, service and fraternal organizations, and so on, may fulfill some social as well as other needs. Junior high school students, who are turning more and more to small groups of their peers for the satisfaction of certain social needs such as companionship and reciprocal affection, might discuss this aspect of group life after reading an excerpt such as this one from *The Adventures of Huckleberry Finn*:

> We went to a clump of bushes, and Tom made everybody swear to keep the secret, and then showed them a hole in the

---

[4] Reprinted from *We Were There on the "Nautilus"* (pp. 154–55), by Robert N. Webb. Copyright © 1961 by Robert N. Webb, published by Grosset & Dunlap, Inc., New York, N.Y.

hill, right in the thickest part of the bushes. Then we lit the candles, and crawled in on our hands and knees. We went about two hundred yards, and then the cave opened up. Tom poked about amongst the passages, and pretty soon ducked under a wall where you wouldn't 'a' noticed that there was a hole. We went along a narrow place and got into a kind of room, all damp and sweaty and cold, and there we stopped. Tom says:

"Now, we'll start this band of robbers and call it Tom Sawyer's Gang. Everybody that wants to join has got to take an oath, and write his name in blood."

Everybody was willing. So Tom got out a sheet of paper that he had wrote the oath on, and read it. It swore every boy to stick to the band, and never tell any of the secrets. . . .

.   .   .   .

Everybody said it was a real beautiful oath, and asked Tom if he got it out of his own head. He said some of it, but the rest was out of pirate books and robber books, and every gang that was high-toned had it.[5]

Numerous literary sources may be employed to help students see that adults as well as children need the satisfactions of peer group companionship. The senior high school teacher, for example, might stimulate meaningful group discussion through the oral reading of this passage from *All Quiet on the Western Front*:

A bomb or something lands close beside me. I have not heard it coming and am terrified. At the same moment a senseless fear takes hold of me. Here I am alone and almost helpless in the dark—. . .

.   .   .   .

There I hear sounds and drop back. Suspicious sounds can be detected clearly despite the noise of the artillery-fire. I listen; the sound is behind me. They are our people moving along the trench. Now I hear muffled voices. To judge by the tone that might be Kat talking.

At once a new warmth flows through me. These voices, these few quiet words, these footsteps in the trench behind me recall me at a bound from the terrible loneliness and fear of death by which I had been almost destroyed. They are more to me than life, these voices, they are more than motherliness and more than fear; they are the strongest, most comforting thing there is anywhere: they are the voices of my comrades.[6]

Also at the senior high school level, the teacher might turn to many telling portions from O. E. Rolvaag's *Giants in the Earth*,

---

[5] Samuel Clemens (New York: Grosset & Dunlap, Inc., 1948), pp. 1–10.

[6] Erich Maria Remarque (London: Putnam & Co., Ltd., 1929), pp. 212, 214–15.

a novel which reveals again and again the pressing need immigrants settling new areas of our country had of each other. This excerpt describes Per Hansa's intense feelings upon finding the trail of the wagon train he must catch to ensure the well-being of his family:

> . . . Sweat was running off him in streams. A quarter of an hour went by; he was still searching frantically. . . . All at once, right at the edge of the woods, he struck a piece of level ground with a larger clearing on it; in the middle of this clearing lay a wide, round patch in the grass. Per Hansa threw himself down on his knees, like a miser who has found a costly treasure; he bent over and sniffed the ground. His blood throbbed; his hands shook as he dug. . . . Yes, he was right—here there had been a fire! It couldn't have been many days ago, either; the smell of the ashes was still fresh. . . . His eyes had grown so moist and dim that he had to wipe them. . . . But he wasn't crying—no, not yet! . . .[7]

Through the literary approach, students may begin to understand representative group functions and assemble lists of functions which groups perform. The teacher might help his students underline the fact that different kinds of groups with varied structures can satisfy the same sorts of human needs.

An alternative to the literary procedure just outlined would be the use of ten to fifteen pictures (easily secured from newspapers, magazines, etc.) showing different groups in action. As with the literary method, this approach could be used at all grade levels. The pictures might include a church congregation singing a hymn, a Boy or Girl Scout meeting in progress, some pupils carrying out a classroom project, members of a family raking leaves in their back yard, a PTA meeting, a political rally, smoke-jumpers fighting a forest fire, a football team listening to a halftime "pep talk," a hobby-club session, people sandbagging a riverbank near their homes in preparation for an impending flood, and so on. The class could then either discuss or write about each of the pictures. In order that students might see that there are many kinds of groups and that groups have particular properties and overlapping and unique functions, they might be guided in their deliberations by questions such as these:

What is happening in this picture?
Why are the people in this group doing what they are doing?

---

[7] *Giants in the Earth: A Saga of the Prairie* (New York: Harper & Row, Publishers, 1927), p. 19.

How many people can you see in the picture? Could *more* people belong to a group like this one? Could *fewer* people belong to such a group?

Can *anyone* belong to a group similar to the one in this picture? Why or why not?

Would everyone *want* to belong to this kind of group? Why or why not?

Have *you* ever belonged to a group like this one? Why or why not?

Could a person belong to this group for *more than one reason?* *Explain* your answer. Give an *example* or two if you can.

Could and would a person belong to this sort of group *all his life?* Why or why not?

Could a person *get along in life* if he belonged only to a group such as this?

Following the discussion or written response stimulated by the pictures, the teacher might invite his class to launch an extensive search for other groups to which people in their community belong. Class members could ask their parents, friends, and others to enumerate as many groups as possible. The "Calendar of Events" columns of a local newspaper might be studied as well. Gradually the investigation could be extended to the national level through an analysis of newspapers, magazines, television offerings, and the like. In some instances, group life in societies outside the United States might be examined and analyzed to see if any of their functions compare with those of groups in America.

A master list of groups might be written on the chalkboard, printed on a large wall chart, or duplicated for everyone's use as a point of embarkation for further class activity. Students could attempt to classify their heterogeneous listings in terms of a variety of criteria. For instance, they could look at the nature of the groups they have enumerated and fit these groups under headings such as *Social, Recreational, Political, Religious,* etc. Or, they might use the scope (local, state-wide, national, international) of groups as a criterion. They could also try to divide groups into primary and secondary relationship categories. Still another possibility would be to see whether groups could be classified by their structure as informal or formal, and so on.

A further possibility inherent in such an endeavor might be to give each pupil one of the groups on the master list and to ask him to share with his classmates his ideas on satisfactions and dissatisfactions, assets and liabilities, or appeals and drawbacks that could be associated with membership in the group assigned to him. Or he might endeavor to evaluate how important that particular group is to its members. After each student has reported, the entire class might try to rank the groups by order of importance, from those that are vital in the daily lives of people on down to those that are less essential or unessential.

Primary grade children traditionally spend a great deal of time studying the most important and universal of all groups, the family. Yet the functions of the family are seldom dealt with in an explicit, reasonably inclusive, realistic fashion. Teachers at this level might help their charges gain some feeling for the significance of the family in our society by having them draw a number of pictures illustrating "Things We Do at Home." While some of the drawings might not be relevant to family living, a large number of them should consist of family-based activities such as playing with brothers and sisters, watching TV with Mom and Dad and others, listening to a story read by Grandma, wrestling with Daddy on the floor, helping Mommy do the dishes, making cookies with Aunt Margaret, washing the car with Cousin Ned, talking with the Welfare Lady, cleaning the house with Mrs. Chandler on Thursdays, etc. The children might also clip out pictures from a variety of magazines to supplement the pictures they have drawn or to help them to express ideas they have trouble communicating in their own drawings and paintings. Illustrations depicting representative family activities would be placed on the bulletin board. The teacher should help children to see that the make-up of families can be quite different and that there is no one, "right" way in which all families must live. Betty Miles' cleverly illustrated children's book, *A House for Everyone*,[8] explores this idea in a way that almost all children can understand. For example, families of varied sizes are portrayed living in a number of types of structures. Similarly, *Where Are the Mothers*,[9] by Dorothy Marino, aids children in perceiving that there is no single manner in which money is earned by the family. (Some mothers stay at home, while others work at a number of occupations.)

Gradually, functions of families could be compared with a few carefully selected groups such as the school class, a Sunday school class, some friends playing together after school, and an audience of children at a Saturday matinee. In these comparisons, the teacher should help pupils to underline unique functions carried out by the family that other groups do not provide for. The children might even attempt to hypothesize about what life would be like *without* families—what would happen to babies if they were left on their

[8] New York: Alfred A. Knopf, Inc., 1958.
[9] New York: J. B. Lippincott Co., 1959.

own after a few months, or what might occur if children had to grow up without any adults at home to help and teach them, and so on. Ultimately, children should be able to understand that the family satisfies many needs that are not generally met by other groups and that patterns of living among families may have some things in common and yet be different in a number of ways.

The teacher who is aware of life-ways in other parts of the world can further expand children's understandings of family structures and functions. For example, among the Hopi the typical pattern is an extended matrilinear family. Long departed ancestors may play an important role in Japanese family life. In *all* families, children are taken care of—sometimes carried around on the mother's back, sometimes watched by other children or by specialized groups as in the Israeli Kibbutz, sometimes cared for by the grandmother as in many Russian families, and so forth.

Perhaps older students might investigate relationships between an individual and one of his groups in a slightly different fashion. Most high school students, for instance, are well aware of the existence of "the gang" in modern, urban America. That many gangs function outside the law is common knowledge; but an understanding of the needs that such gangs fulfill for some young people is less apt to be grasped meaningfully. The teacher might use portions of a study such as Lewis Yablonsky's *The Violent Gang* to approach this kind of understanding. Yablonsky describes the factors that led a young Puerto Rican immigrant to become a member of a particular group:

> Jose's family was of little help to him in New York. Their rules, language and appearance were "old fashioned." Also, his parents and older brothers were busy battling their own enemies in the city. Jose's family was generally not around. . . . In the old days, Jose had the opportunity and would discuss his personal troubles with his parents and older relatives. It was even pleasant to be criticized, since it gave Jose a secure feeling to know someone was concerned. In the park, not only his own parents but also relatives and other adults took an interest in children. One man took the boys swimming; a group of older men from a social club formed a baseball league for the younger boys. Jose belonged to a community.
> All of this changed in New York.
> Jose one day met a violent gang leader called Loco. Although many neighborhood youths, including the Braves, thought he was crazy, his reputation for sudden violence through the use of a knife or a zip gun made him greatly feared. Loco, at the time, as part of his usual gang leader activity, was "organizing" a West Side Dragon's Division. Jose was

accepted without question and was appointed a war counselor by Loco after he saw him "in action." Loco saw Jose stab a younger boy on a dare.

. . . .

The Kings provided a vehicle for expressing much of the hatred, disillusionment, and aggression that existed in Jose. . . . The gang helped minimize feelings of guilt and anxiety about violence at the rare times such feelings existed. Acting out violence with gang compatriots was more satisfying than doing it alone. Any limited concern he had with feelings of worthlessness were diminished by the recognition that there were others as "loyal" as himself.[10]

Following the reading of this case history, students might be asked to compare Jose's earlier life with their own. Were there similarities, differences? Have they ever experienced similar feelings? What was missing from Jose's environment that led to his joining the gang? What did this group do for him? What did it do *to* him? What was its purpose, its function? It should eventually become clear that Jose's basic desire for group membership, recognition, and respect is normal and universal, but, because of a variety of circumstances, the group from which he eventually gained satisfaction was destructive rather than constructive in nature.

Students at a variety of age levels might gather empirical data dealing with their own individual and group activities over a period of time. For example, a high school class could be asked to keep a record of things they do as individuals and those they do as group members during a succession of high school days. The students might find that they occasionally work in class committees, attend after-school clubs, participate in student government, are members of a school newspaper, etc. A class composite of such group activities would reveal that most high school students spend surprisingly large amounts of their time in a variety of group activities that serve a number of purposes.

2. A Society Exists in the Minds of Its Members and Occurs Only When There Is Communication or Interaction Among Those Members. The Mere Grouping or Aggregating of People Does Not Produce a Society.

The essence of a society cannot be found in the physical appearance of its members or in the natural properties of the

---

[10] New York: The Macmillan Co., 1962; pp. 165–68.

place they inhabit. A society does not consist of fair skin, freckles, green eyes, and red hair, or lofty peaks, verdant valleys, sleepy lagoons, satin-smooth beaches, swaying palm trees, exotic flowers, and balmy breezes. The real substance of a society consists of the ideas its members hold and share. The individuals in a group may be of different sizes, shapes, and colors; but if they exchange thoughts and feelings (communicate) and mutually adjust their behavior (interact) they are a society. A society may have few or many members, may have a brief or extended existence, may have the same location or be transported to other locations in the minds of its members.

The second generalization we have drawn from the preceding five chapters by Mrs. Rose has a number of methodological possibilities. This fundamental sociological observation could be approached initially through an exploration of the idea of society itself at differing conceptual levels. The elementary teacher, for instance, might invite the children to play a game with him where no one in the class would talk for ten minutes and where pupils would respond to various gestures made by the teacher. The teacher could begin the game by stepping out of the room for a moment and then entering with a big smile on his face and a friendly wave of his hand. The children would return the smile and the gesture of greeting. Next, the teacher might shake hands enthusiastically with everyone. Following the handshaking, the teacher could put up both fists and look angrily at the class as if "trying to pick a fight." Then he might signal for everyone to rise and to sit down again by lifting and lowering both arms. He could then nod his head up and down and turn it from side to side to stimulate corresponding "yes" and "no" responses from the group, etc. After the game has been concluded, the teacher would ask the children to discuss the *meaning* of each of the gestures and *how they knew what to do* when they observed the motions.

At this point, the teacher would ask his charges to imagine that they have been dropped suddenly into a land where people use gestures instead of speaking. The motions the people employ include the same ones that were incorporated into the game played in class, *but they mean just the opposite things!* The youngsters would then be asked to discuss problems they might encounter in this new situation in expressing their wants and ideas and in understanding the fictitious inhabitants. Gradually the children could be lead to the perception that as a result of their membership in a particular society they have learned certain gestures and other forms of expression and behavior which make it possible for them to communicate and interact with others who belong to their society. Class members could see, too, that things they have learned in one society could make it difficult for them to interact with human beings who have a different societal background and orientation. With a group of carefully selected illustrations and the teacher's assistance, however, the children should understand that an individual can learn the ways of another society and can even become a functioning member of more than one society. Through their exposure to pictures, slides, filmstrips, films, stories, accounts, etc., from societies in different parts of the world, pupils might see as well that gestures and other forms of expression, customs, thoughts, beliefs, and values are part of the communication and interaction patterns of every society, though they may differ from society to society.

In a similar vein, children and youth at most instructional levels could examine *why* societies have developed unique forms of communication and interaction.[11] For example, the teacher might tell the story of Helen Keller's life and read excerpts from William Gibson's poignant play *The Miracle Worker*.[12] The teacher should concentrate on the idea that Helen had to learn a system of communication and a way of interacting meaningfully with her fellow human beings in order to develop the skills we have come to call "intelligence," as well as to become a functioning member of her family society in particular and American society in general. Teachers will find especially valuable for purposes of class discussion the moving passage describing the moment Helen first connects the symbols her teacher, Annie Sullivan, has been pressing constantly into her hand with *real* objects in her own world. This occurs, the reader may recall, when Annie spells the word "water" into Helen's hand as they fill a pitcher at the water pump.

An awareness of some differences existing between a communicating, interacting group and a mere collection of persons can be developed with even relatively young children through a simple teaching procedure involving the use of carefully selected discussion pictures arranged in pairs. The first pair of pictures might include a PTA meeting and a group of "sidewalk superintendents" watching a construction job in progress. Pair number two could consist of an elementary school class working on a project and

---

[11] A study of this question might also help students to develop some insight into the even larger question of why societies have been and are formed. The teacher could utilize a number of perspectives here, including the historical, political, geographic, economic, religious, social, scientific, and technological.

[12] New York: Atheneum Publishers, 1960; pp. 295–97.

hundreds of people walking towards a baseball or football stadium. The next duo might compare a family engaged in a dinner-time discussion with a number of persons waiting on a platform for a subway train, etc. In each case the class would be asked to look for differences between the groups of people in the paired combinations; to point out what is happening in *all* of the "first" pictures (the PTA meeting, the elementary school class, and the family) that is *not* happening in the companion photographs. It would be apparent to children that people are together in all of the illustrations, but they would be pressed to identify as many contrasts as possible between the first and second columns. Then the youngsters might be asked to think of ways in which the latter groups could become more like the former. (For instance, the people watching the construction work might start talking to each other about the project, might decide to continue their conversation over a cup of coffee in a cafe across the street, might originate an idea which would improve the efficiency of the workmen and save the construction company money, and might go across the street again together to share their thoughts with a foreman.)

Another aspect of the fundamental perception under discussion is the idea that people of different backgrounds, abilities, interests, and persuasions can develop, through communication and interaction, common and shared meanings and thus make for a functioning society. This understanding is particularly important in a democratic, pluralistic society (though it has important international overtones as well) and can and should be handled in various ways. In grades three through six, the teacher might start a project illustrating this idea through children's collections of bubble-gum cards picturing athletes on the same professional baseball or football team. First the cards could be pinned on a bulletin board face up. A general discussion of the team and its performance for the season might ensue for a few minutes. Then all of the cards could be turned over and pinned to the board again. This time each of the biographical sketches appearing on the cards could be read aloud by different members of the class. It would soon be obvious that the players were born in various states, had differing amounts of education, and attended a number of colleges and universities, may even have had former loyalties as a result of playing for one or more other professional teams before joining their present organization, and the like. At this point the teacher could ask how it is possible for men with different backgrounds to become members of a close, smoothly operating group. Children who know their sports could point out that the players are continually coached, have secret signals to call for pitches and plays (communication), and spend hours in locker rooms and training sessions trading ideas and adjusting their mutual behavior (interaction) to improve their play.

Students at various educational levels might be shown a picture of a famous jazz combo or a full symphony orchestra, where individuals of different experiential bases, sizes, shapes, colors, etc., have worked tirelessly together to achieve tonal effects that give the impression of a single voice. Older students might be asked to thumb through publications like *Who's Who in America* and to observe the highly heterogeneous group of individuals who have been included in this source because of their prominence in and/or contribution to American society. Or, the teacher might ask each student to write a brief biographical sketch on one member of the United States Senate so individual differences in this legislative group could be compared and discussed. Still another possibility would be for the class to examine biographical notes on opera and play programs to see that the talents of persons with different backgrounds have been tapped to achieve an artistic purpose. American society as a whole and many of its smaller societies taken separately exemplify in manifest ways the idea sketched here. The general procedures outlined for this aspect of our second sociological concept could be used at the international level as well, of course, with materials dealing with activities of the United Nations, a world convention of mathematicians or scientists, and so on.

Whatever his approach, the teacher could point out that the *medium* (athletics, music, public service, politics, drama, diplomacy, mathematics, science, etc.) of communication or interaction might vary but that very different people who share purposes and who care can form, improve, and preserve innumerable kinds of societies.

Another facet of our second major idea from sociology concerns the notion that society cannot exist without *man*: societies arise out of human needs and conditions, and societies are being born constantly. To expose younger children to an element of this understanding, the primary teacher might read aloud to the class the story *What Was I Scared Of?* by Dr. Seuss.[13] This brief tale deals with a little character who is afraid of an active pair of empty green pants. After trying to avoid the pants, he finds himself standing face to face with them, and he hollers for help. He finds, however, that the pants are just as frightened as he; and he and the pants become friends. While this Seuss story seems to be concerned primarily with fear of the unknown, it could be used as

[13] Dr. Seuss, *The Sneetches: And Other Stories* (New York: Random House, Inc., 1961), pp. 42–65.

well to help children see how people unknown to each other can become acquainted, and friendships can lead to the formation of groups. The classroom discussion could be expanded easily into the sharing of ideas as to how strangers placed in a group situation may evolve into a society. Examples from colonial, pioneer, and contemporary life could be suggested by the teacher and the children. The word "society" might be introduced and some simple sociological details brought into focus.

A teacher in grades one through six might invite a kindergarten colleague down the hall to serve as a resource person to help "bigger, more experienced" children gain some feeling for the emergent nature of a society. Initially, the kindergarten teacher could tell the "older" pupils in a detailed and humorous fashion about a "typical" first day in a kindergarten classroom. First-day tears, fights, struggles over toys and turns on the slide, shouting across the room, sleepy spells, and the like, might be mentioned. Then the resource person could explain in a step-by-step manner how the lonesome, confused, self-centered kindergarten children learn over the months to share needs, thoughts, and feelings and mutually adjust their behavior so they become welded into a "little society." After a question and discussion period with the kindergarten teacher, class members could be helped by their regular teacher to expand and transfer the kindergarten illustration to other societal settings.

Junior or senior high school students might role-play a situation which deals with the formation of a short-lived society. The problem story employed might be something like this:

It is almost 10:00 P.M. on a Friday night at New York's Kennedy Airport. A huge jet airplane is being loaded for a flight to San Francisco. All the reservations for this flight have been taken. Four men are waiting at the airline ticket counter in the airport to see if passengers holding reservations on the flight will fail to show up so they can get on board. The four men arrived at the airport on the same limousine and came simultaneously to the counter, so no one has preference. The airline clerk has been too busy getting ticketed passengers ready for loading to talk with the four men about their reasons for making the flight. He knows only that all of them would like to have a seat on the plane. The four men have been standing at the counter for almost twenty minutes. They have not conversed. The next flight to San Francisco does not leave until 7:20 A.M. Finally, the airline clerk tells the men that one passenger ticketed for the flight has not appeared and that they must decide among them which one of the four will take the flight.

Each of the four students taking part in this sociodramatic activity would receive a 3" x 5" card as an orientation for the role-playing. The cards could read as follows:

First Man: You are a young second lieutenant in the United States Army. You are going home on furlough. You have not seen your family or your fiancé for two years. Tomorrow night your family is going to have a welcome-home dinner for you. You are very anxious to get home. This is the flight you want to take, but through a mix-up you were ticketed for the 7:20 flight in the morning.

Second Man: You are an outstanding eye surgeon who specializes in a particular kind of delicate operation. A physician in San Francisco who is familiar with your work called you just two hours ago. He asked you to fly west right away so you could perform an emergency operation on a little boy who may lose his sight if he does not receive prompt attention.

Third Man: You are beginning a two weeks' vacation. You had planned to stay at home this year, but at the last minute you decided to fly to San Francisco for a change of scenery. You were too late to get a reservation on the evening flight, but you decided to take a chance on a cancellation. You finished an exhausting week at 5:30 P.M. today, and you would really like to get away from it all.

Fourth Man: You are the national sales manager for a large company. Your regional salesman in the Bay Area called you this afternoon to see if you could help him with a big deal tomorrow morning. You are supposed to be in the customer's office at 9:30 sharp. The customer intends to place a huge order very soon with your company or with your biggest competitor. He likes prompt service.

Following the enactment, the entire class could discuss the sequence of events that would transform four complete strangers into a small, temporary society. Students could examine how each individual identified his own situation and became aware of the problems facing the others. The class could observe the communication and interaction among the four men, the decision-making procedures employed by the quartet, and the nature of the agreement reached by the miniature society. The members of the class would see the competing needs that can be present in a society and the accommodation that can take place. Students could be asked to note that the four men were not a society before the incident and that they would no longer be a society after they have resolved the specific issue facing them. Other dimensions of sociological generalizations could be developed with this same procedure.

With respect to our second key idea from sociology, we have said that a society exists in the minds of its members, that the essence of a society is embodied in the ideas its members hold and share. We believe that this is a crucial understanding for contemporary man and that portions of the many things it implies can be explored by children and youth. At the elementary level the teacher might employ a story such as *Little Navajo Bluebird* by Ann Nolan Clark to help children see that a person—in this instance a child, appropriately—can carry a mental image of a society with him even though he may move to a different place or associate himself with a different society. The passages quoted below deal with a little Navajo girl, Hobah, who decides to leave her family for a time to attend the White Man's school but who wants very much to remember and keep the ways of her people and to return to them. Her big brother hurt her parents deeply when he went away to school and did not return. Her father wants to make sure that he does not lose his beloved little girl and takes special precautions to help her retain her society's ideas and beliefs.

> Then a strange thing happened. A look of wanting came to Hobah's eyes, an excited, eager look of wanting. "School is good, I think," she said. "When I go I will learn the new things to help make the old things better. Always will I be a daughter of the People, but I want to have much wisdom, knowing many ways. There is good, some good, in all things, I think." Pride lived in the deep dark eyes of Elder Sister. Doli saw and understood. Hobah's mind would seek new knowledge, but her feet would stay firmly in the footprints of her mother's trail.
>
> . . . .
>
> Miles away, Father rode steadily. He rode with a purpose. His goal was the hogan of Dawn Singer, Navajo Medicine Man. If his daughter must go within the White Man's world, let her go prepared! Never again would a child of his go forth alone into that strange country. Hobah would take with her Holy Medicine whose power would keep her untouched by strange ways so that, School ended, she would return to him.
>
> . . . .

At last Hobah spoke, "Little Bluebird, my younger Sister, do not grieve that today I leave you. I am of the People. Always will I return to the People. Look, my Sister! I give you this to keep for me until I return. It is my most precious possession. Take it." She handed Doli her garnet stone, gift from the Yei.[14]

From the intermediate grades through the senior high school, students might be challenged to uncover their own examples of real people who have demonstrated through their actions that they have internalized ideas, beliefs, and values of one or more societies. In their study of American history, for example, young people might come across the story of Captain William Wells, a man who truly understood two ways of life and carried these understandings with him from one place to the other. Wells lived among the Indians and was the adopted son of Little Turtle. He fought on the Indian side at Harmar's and St. Clair's defeats. Wells also headed a corps of spies under "Mad Anthony" Wayne and provided Wayne with valuable information on the ways of Ohio tribesmen. After serving Wayne, Wells lived the rest of his life with the Indians. Or, students might look at the period of heavy immigration in the United States and note how many newcomers to America brought elements of their societies with them and lived according to some customs and standards that were part of another culture. Students could even find some contemporary examples of parts of cities where people of German or Italian or Chinese extraction live and retain societal learnings other than those common in their surroundings.

Senior high school students might search in their study of current events for illustrations of the existence of society in the minds of its members. One compelling case occurs in Peru where two distinct societies exist in spite of the fact that all the people are Peruvians. *Time* magazine carried a story—an excerpt of which appears below—which could be used to stimulate discussion and a quest for similar examples.

This is Indian South America, land of the ancient Incas and Spanish *conquistadores*, whose 45 million descendants have always lived in mutually exclusive societies: the white Spanish minority that owns the wealth and the hopeless, anonymous Indian and half-breed majority that exists in squalid slums or labors on Andean haciendas. "In the sweep of all its

---

[14] From *Little Navajo Bluebird* (pp. 37, 70, 77), by Ann Nolan Clark. Copyright 1943, by Ann Nolan Clark and Paul Lantz. Reprinted by permission of The Viking Press, Inc.

history," says Belaunde, "our land has been the theater of endless bloody struggles. And always there remained great gulfs between the conquerors and the conquered."

Belaunde intends to bridge the gulfs not so much by taking from the rich but by giving the peasant masses a stake in their country through massive social reforms and self-help development programs. He offers more food, better jobs, new roads, schools, hospitals, industries. He reminds the Indians of the Inca civilization that once flourished in Peru, talks of "a new renaissance," and challenges them to enlist in what he calls "the conquest of Peru by Peruvians."[15]

3. Man Is a Flexible, Becoming Creature. Through the Socialization Process, He Can Learn Approved Ways of Behaving in a Variety of Societies.

The biological inheritance of *Homo sapiens* both necessitates and facilitates socialization. When the wonderful, lovable bundle of needs and potentialities we call a *baby* first joins the human procession, he is helpless for a long period of time. He cannot survive in isolation, and through his associations with others he learns from them. All ways of living in groups are learned. An infant is so magnificently plastic that he is capable of becoming a successful member of countless societies, small and large, simple and complex. He is not innately an American, a Californian, a Republican, a Methodist, or a San Francisco Giants fan. He becomes any of these things through learning, and, as a result of his continued interactions with other persons, he slowly, gradually, sometimes joyfully or painfully develops into a performing, responsive, and responsible member of a society.

Societies appear and disappear, grow and atrophy, change and resist change, satisfy and fail to satisfy the needs of their members. A particular society may mean many things to many people. But any established society, regardless of its condition or connotations, must have some degree of consistency in its expectations and behavioral patterns in order to achieve its aims and assure its continuation. In certain instances, then, there are forms of behavior in specified societal situations that can be anticipated or predicted. The more complex a society is, the more likely it is that it will employ a larger number of agencies and institutions to socialize its members and the more difficult it is to examine and assess the influence of forces at play in the socialization of individuals.

---

[15] "Peru: The New Conquest," *Time,* XXCV, No. 11 (March 12, 1965), 32. Courtesy of *Time;* copyright Time, Inc., 1965.

Socialization—the process by which society gets into the minds of people—warrants continued attention at various levels of instruction, in our opinion. We believe that an understanding of and appreciation for the socialization process can give students greater self-insight and social sensitivity. The patient discovery, extended study, and creative application of such insights can nourish more objective and meaningful views of other societies and lead toward a more cosmopolitan perspective of mankind. And, there is a chance that contact with similar perceptions might give birth to a certain balanced optimism when young people find that man's die is not completely cast, but that alterations have taken and can take place in his social behavior.

There are innumerable literary selections that teachers could read aloud to their pupils or have their students read prior to a discussion of dimensions of the socialization process. A teacher of primary youngsters, for example, might read aloud a book such as *Taro and the Tōfu* by Masako Matsuno.[16] The Japanese setting adds an appealing touch to a value-oriented problem situation which is meaningful to small children. Taro, a small Japanese boy, faces a difficult decision when the tōfu (a bean curd cake) seller gives him back forty yen too much in change after a purchase. The boy is already at the candy store when he discovers the error. Should he buy an extra treat or return the money? Children could be asked at first to talk about what they think Taro will do and *why* they believe their responses are correct. Then the conclusion to the story might be read. Again, the class could explain why they feel Taro made the decision he did and what they would do under similar circumstances and why. Gradually class members could be invited to focus their exchange of ideas upon how people learn what is expected of them and what to do under a variety of circumstances and in many settings. Eventually the teacher could turn to the chalkboard and ask his pupils to suggest a number of things they have learned and to try to think of where and when they learned them and who taught them. A large list could be made so children would be confronted with a fairly representative sample of social understandings and values that have been transmitted to them. Class members might also see the diverse sources for certain learnings.

A primary teacher might read *Charlotte's Web* by E. B. White [17] and ask his charges to listen for things that Charlotte the spider teaches Wilbur the pig and Templeton the rat. Following a listing of a group of Charlotte's precepts, admonishments,

---

[16] Cleveland: The World Publishing Co., 1962.
[17] New York: Harper & Row, Publishers, 1952.

etc., the children could then talk about people who have been important in their lives and who have instructed them in the ways of their society.

Mary Jane Carr's *Young Mac of Fort Vancouver* is something of a study in socialization and could be read to or by pupils in the intermediate grades. The story deals with Donald MacDermott, whose father was a Scott and whose mother was an Indian. The reader follows Donald from childhood to manhood and witnesses many varied societal expectations to which he is exposed. A passage such as the one which appears below could be discussed at some length in class and then followed up with contemporary illustrations brought forth by class members. This excerpt comes at the conclusion of a section which describes a trip the thirteen-year-old Donald makes with the *voyageurs* of the York Factory Express from St. Andrew's in Prince Rupert's Land to Fort Vancouver.

> "Tomorrow," said Henri, "Young Mac's first voyage comes to an end at Fort Vancouver. A long, hard journey, it was, and he complained not once. He took his place at the paddle with the best of you. On the long portage he carried his heavy pack like a man. He ate the greasy rubaboo without grumble, and when there was nothing in the pots for supper, he pulled his belt tighter, and said not a word, though all his growing bones cried out for food. He sat tight when the canoes shot rapids, and sang to keep up our spirits. Not even at the *Dalles des Morts* (Canyon of the Dead) where the tall white crosses tell of boatmen who died in the boiling water, did he falter. Did any of you see him falter?"
>
> "*Non! Non!*"
>
> "Now you have just seen him frighten a timber wolf to death. Is he not one of us? Is Young Mac not a Northman?"
>
> "*Oui! Oui!*" the voyageurs shouted: "Yes! Yes! Behold Young Mac, the Northman!"
>
> "You have learned the creed of the voyageur," Henri said to Donald. "The creed that has made the sons of the fur trade able to look death in the face without flinching; to know fear, as all men must know fear, but not to be conquered by fear. To be able to think clearly and quickly. To keep a high heart. It is voted that you have earned the right to wear the feather of a Northman." . . .[18]

The teacher could use Kipling's classic *Captains Courageous* to help intermediate children trace and discuss the implications of the abrupt socialization and drastic transformation of Harvey

---

[18] From: *Young Mac of Fort Vancouver*, pp. 25–26. Copyright 1940 by Mary Jane Carr. Reprinted by permission of the publishers, Thomas Y. Crowell Company, New York.

Cheyne, the wealthy, spoiled boy who falls off an ocean liner and is rescued by the crew of a fishing schooner, thereby moving from his previous society to a very different one. Passages such as these could be used to stimulate reactions from the class:

> "Ah ha!" said Manuel, holding out a brown hand. "You are some pretty well now? This time last night the fish they fish for you. Now you fish for fish. Eh, wha-at?"
>
> "I'm—I'm ever so grateful," Harvey stammered, and his unfortunate hand stole to his pocket once more, but he remembered that he had no money to offer. When he knew Manuel better the mere thought of the mistake he might have made would cover him with hot, uneasy blushes in his bunk.
>
> "There is no to be thankful for to *me!*" said Manuel. "How shall I leave you dreef, dreef all around the Banks? Now you are a fisherman—eh, wha-at?"
>
> .   .   .   .
>
> . . . The boys were tired long ere the halibut, who took charge of them and the dory for the next twenty minutes. But the big flat fish was gaffed and hauled in at last.
>
> "Beginner's luck," said Dan, wiping his forehead. "He's all of a hundred."
>
> Harvey looked at the huge gray-and-mottled creature with unspeakable pride. He had seen halibut many times on marble slabs ashore, but it had never occurred to him to ask how they came inland. Now he knew; and every inch of his body ached with fatigue.[19]

At the intermediate or secondary levels, the teacher should be able to elicit a worthwhile, sensitive commentary from students through the reading of an excerpt like the following from *My Little Boy*, by the Danish novelist Carl Ewald:

> There is great warfare and a lot of noise among the children in the yard.
>
> I hear them yell *Jew*. I go to the window and see my little boy bareheaded out in the front line of the battle.
>
> I settle down quietly to my work again, certain that he will appear shortly and tell me all about it.
>
> Soon after he is there.
>
> He stands next to me, as is his habit, and says nothing. I steal a glance at him—he is highly excited, feels very proud and happy, like one who has fearlessly done his duty.
>
> "Such fun you had down there."
>
> "Well," he says modestly, "—it was only a Jewish boy we were beating up."

---

[19] Rudyard Kipling (New York: Bantam Books, Inc., 1896), pp. 20–21, 34.

I jump up so my chair turns over.

"A Jewish boy—you were beating him up—what had he done?"

"Nothing."

His voice is not very confident, for I look so queer.

But this is only the beginning. For now I grab my hat and run out the door as fast as I can and yell:

"Come on—come on—we must find him and ask his forgiveness."

My little boy hurries after me. He does not understand a word but he is terribly in earnest. We look in the yard, we shout and yell. We rush into the street and around the corner. Breathlessly we ask three people if they have seen a poor, mistreated Jewish boy.

All in vain. The Jewish boy and all the persecutors have vanished.

"Well—," I say, "there is nothing more we can do. I hope you will meet that boy some day, so you can shake hands with him and ask him to forgive you. You must tell him that you did it because you were stupid, that if anyone tries to harm him again, you will help him and beat them as long as you can stir a limb."

.   .   .   .

"Let me tell you—the Jews are very wonderful people. You remember David whom Dirty read about in school? He was a Jewish boy. And Jesus whom everybody worships and loves although he died two thousand years ago. He was also Jewish."

My little boy rests his arms on my knees and I go on with my story.

The old Hebrews rise before our eyes with a splendor and power quite different from Dirty's Catechism. They ride on their camels in their colorful clothing and with their long beards. . . Moses and Joseph and his brothers and Samson and David and Saul. Wonderful stories these are. The walls of Jericho fall before the blast of the trumpets. . . .

.   .   .   .

My little boy is hot and flustered when he goes to sleep that night. Restlessly he tosses in his bed and talks in his sleep.

"He is a bit feverish," his mother says.

"No wonder. Today I vaccinated him against the meanest of all common blights." [20]

It should be obvious to students hearing this passage that the father hopes to help his son grow up without being racially prejudiced. Students could understand as well that prejudice is

[20] New York: Horizon Press, Inc., 1962, pp. 81–85.

learned and that those people who are prejudiced were not born that way but were taught hate. At this point the teacher might turn to the recording of the musical play *South Pacific* for another illustration in a somewhat different context. The class could listen to and discuss the dramatic moment at which Lieutenant Cable bitterly observes that one is not *born* with racial prejudice—rather, as the song says, "you've got to be *taught* to hate and fear . . ., you've got to be carefully taught." [21]

Another play which is unusually perceptive and which could be excerpted by the teacher to stimulate thinking about the socialization process is *The Teahouse of the August Moon,* with its setting in Okinawa. This passage—delivered at the beginning of the play by Sakini, an interpreter serving the American occupation forces—reveals that the Okinawans have been "socialized" by a group of outside forces and that what one accepts as normal and proper behavior is very much a product of what he·has been taught in a given societal situation:

> History of Okinawa reveals distinguished record of conquerors.
> We have honor to be subjugated in fourteenth century by Chinese pirates.
> In sixteenth century by English missionaries.
> In eighteenth century by Japanese war lords.
> And in twentieth century by American Marines.
> Okinawa very fortunate.
> Culture brought to us. . . . Not have to leave home for it.
> Learn many things.
> Most important that rest of world not like Okinawa.
> World filled with delightful variation.
> Illustration.
> In Okinawa . . . no locks on doors.
> Bad manners not to trust neighbors.
> In America . . . lock and key big industry.
> Conclusion?
> Bad manners good business.[22]

In a slightly different vein—focusing not so much upon the socialization process itself as upon the capacity of man to become a functioning member of a myriad of societies—children in the intermediate grades might be asked to write out their own answers to questions constructed around a fictitious story such as this one:

---

[21] Richard Rodgers and Oscar Hammerstein, 2nd, *South Pacific: A Musical Play* (New York: Random House, Inc., 1949), pp. 136–37.

[22] Reprinted by permission of G. P. Putnam's Sons, from *Teahouse of the August Moon* (p. 8), by John Patrick. Copyright 1955 by John Patrick.

Harry Mitchell and Betty Rankin were married after they were graduated from the same college. Mr. Mitchell started his own little hardware and appliance store in Seattle, Washington, and business was good. Mr. and Mrs. Mitchell liked children, but they did not have any boys or girls of their own. They decided to adopt a baby, and their minister helped them adopt a Korean orphan. Now the girl is a sixth grader in a Seattle elementary school.

The teacher could construct questions like the following:

What language do you think the girl would speak?
How might she dress?
What foods do you believe she would like best?
What do you believe she might do after school?
What do you think she will do when she grows up?
What country might she love the most?

The children will probably realize instantly that the girl would have learned the ways of her parents and the American society of which she is a member. Some children might observe that the girl could know very little or perhaps nothing about the place of her birth, its customs, and values. A few youngsters could suggest that a child born in any country and raised in another one by people who embrace the way of life of the second locale would learn and internalize the expectations transmitted to him.

With secondary students, a teacher might ask each student in the class to choose the name of one person listed on the chalkboard, to read carefully about that individual, and then to present an oral report to the class on the life of the person selected. The teacher could suggest that his students pay particular attention to the family life and education of the individual, though this probably would not be necessary to achieve the desired purpose. These are just a few names which the teacher might use:

Charles Proteus Steinmetz	Arturo Toscanini
Albert Einstein	Alexander Procofieff DeSeversky
Joseph Pulitzer	Irving Berlin
Alexander Graham Bell	Alexander Hamilton
Andrew Carnegie	Bruno Walter

In the cases of the men identified above and those of many other individuals who could be cited for this purpose, students would discover that there were significant adjustments involved from at least one society to another. Bruno Walter, for example, was born in Germany, became a French citizen, and finally became an American citizen.

Or, a person in the school community who is truly bilingual and who has lived for a substantial period of time in at least two societies might be invited to talk to a secondary class as a resource person. This guest could talk about the many things he had to learn about the approved ways of behaving in the different societies, the assistance he received, and the problems he faced.

Finally, Mary Ellen Chase, in her autobiographical *The White Gate,* writes a poignant account of the development of social sensitivity in a young child that offers many possibilities for discussion and elaboration at a variety of grade levels. The author's parents, assuming the child is asleep, happily discuss plans for her birthday the next day. The child cannot help overhearing their excited talk, and, as she listens, these thoughts run through her mind:

> I was tense from two emotions as I lay there, emotions so real that I have never forgotten them. The first was an almost guilty terror lest they should discover I was awake when I should have been fast asleep and reprove me as for some misbehavior. But the second, when it seized me, was so much stronger than the first that, after a few breathless moments of fear, it quite ousted the first from my imagination. What really tormented me as I lay there was the necessity of guarding my mother and Do from the knowledge I was aware of their secret. For I suddenly realized as I listened to them whispering and laughing together, in the lamplight, by the table, that older people sometimes had secrets also, which they held sacred as did children. In a strange way, too, on that evening when I was just leaving eight for nine years old, I understood that older people might be children also. My mother and Do had always before seemed old to me, but as I lay there listening, I knew all at once that they were also young and that I must protect *them* from disappointment and regret, guard *their* secret, preserve *their* happiness from ruin.[23]

4. *The Interdependence of Groups in a Complex Contemporary Society Serves as a Bond Which Holds That Society Together.*

The members of a modern society are greatly dependent upon one another for the satisfaction of many of their basic and acquired

---

[23] New York: W. W. Norton & Co., Inc., 1954; pp. 77–78.

needs. As a society grows in size and in the functions it performs, it spins a more and more intricate web of human interrelationships. And as man becomes increasingly specialized, he relies to a greater extent upon his neighbors near and far for countless goods and services. During a given day in his existence, he may be protected, sheltered, fed, clothed, guided, taught, informed, and helped by many people. In one sense, he plays fewer solos on life's stage and more ensemble renditions as a musician in a huge orchestra. In another sense, however, specialization enables some people to become "stars," i.e., to excel in a given, limited field. In the simple rural community where constant back-breaking labor is necessary merely to keep alive, the development of the great artist or virtuoso is exceedingly difficult.

The idea of mutual dependence and its function as a form of societal "mortar" can be critically and creatively considered through the use of many methodological procedures. This fourth sociological generalization will blend in nicely with a group of current curricular offerings in our schools, and it can be utilized in projected program planning in districts engaged in revision efforts. In current courses of study, for example, this basic idea could be approached in the primary grades as a part of an enlightened examination of community helpers. In the intermediate grades, aspects of early colonial life in America and feudal life in Europe could be related to this generalization. During the junior high school years, students could see forms of interdependence evident in many topics and themes treated in geography, in industrialization and the birth of cities, and in civic and governmental activities. And, in the senior high school, there are abundant opportunities to deal with mutual dependence in the world and the United States yesterday and today, in issues and problems spotlighted for study, in economics, and, of course, in sociology. This sociological idea would obviously be compatible with a more systematic, structured approach as well. Hence, there are various possibilities for the use and methodological interpretation of this generalization.

Primary children might be exposed to the idea of interdependence by being asked to think of things they need and use every day and to identify as many people as they can on whom they depend for these important things in their lives. The teacher could write the people suggested on the chalkboard and then invite a discussion of the unique and combined functions these persons perform. The following are a few items that the children might list:

mothers	food processors	salespeople
fathers	clothing manufacturers	newspaper and
grandparents	workers in plants	television people
other relatives	and mills	policemen
grocery men	carpenters	firemen
milkmen	plumbers	doctors
farmers	electricians	shipping employees
fishermen	sanitation men	teachers
loggers	power company men	librarians
truck drivers	telephone men	janitors
railroad men	bus drivers	barbers
airline employees	service station operators	nurses

To expand the idea of interdependence, the teacher could have each child volunteer to take one of the items listed on the chalkboard and to find out how that single classification of people (that is, farmers, truck drivers, service station operators, etc.) is dependent upon other groups of persons. Children could read about some groups, ask their parents about others, and perhaps interview still others. After each child has shared his findings with the class, the children might construct a device to help them visualize lines of interrelationships. For example, each child might print a round disk identifying his group of people which would be placed on the bulletin board. Every pupil would have his own pieces of yarn in a distinct color which he could fasten to those disks where a dependent relationship exists. Eventually the board would be a colorful hodgepodge, revealing dramatically that each of us is dependent upon many others for the satisfaction of his various needs.

At the secondary level, a classroom teacher could employ a procedure that bears some resemblance to the method outlined above. However, he might approach the idea of interdependence by moving his class from the general to the particular instead of from the particular to the general as was suggested in the primary-oriented illustration. Using a problem situation like the one sketched below, he could have each of his students originate an independent written response as a homework assignment which would then be brought to class and discussed by the total group.

You are a multi-millionaire who has amassed a tremendous fortune in heavy industry. As an investment a number of years ago, you purchased a huge expanse of land in the Southwest. You have been so busy for such a long time that you had almost forgotten about this tract. You do not need the money which would come from the sale of this property. Your beloved wife passed away five years ago, and you have no other living relatives. You feel that you owe a great deal to America for the many opportunities it has given you, and you are deeply devoted to democratic ideals. You have always been a generous man and have contributed widely to various humane causes. But you would like to do something really special for your fellow citizens which will be dedicated to your wife's memory. You decide to create what you think would be an ideal community for younger married couples and their children on the site in the Southwest. You will provide the land and two million dollars which can be used for materials that will be needed to start the construction of some public buildings.

You estimate that your property will accommodate comfortably around 7,000 men, women, and children. You will have to work out some system for distributing residential lots which will be fair to the people who apply. Also, the land you are going to use for this project is fifty-two miles away from the nearest city of any size, which would make commuting difficult and costly for the people in this community, so it would have to be composed of people who could provide many of the necessary goods and services. This does not bother you, for you see this is an ideal opportunity to put a group of fine people together who can help each other live a good and complete life. You have friends in business who might consider starting branch plants and offices in this locale. The most important problem, you believe, is the selection of residents from the large group of applicants you anticipate. Assuming you have a considerable variety of applicants, attempt to select the first fifty by occupation.

Secondary students should see, with little or no assistance from the teacher, that there would be a great deal of mutual dependence in this community which would require people with a variety of abilities and skills. They might understand that heterogeneity is essential for more complex societies, since so many different tasks must be performed. They should be able to perceive eventually that the interdependence demanded in this fictional situation would serve as a bond that would closely unite residents.

Another approach could be appropriately adjusted to instructional levels ranging from the third through the sixth grades. This procedure could be employed by teachers located where a given urban community and a particular rural community are reasonably close to each other and have established definite, identifiable patterns of mutual dependence. The underlying purpose of this approach would be to help youngsters become familiar with a group of goods and services required and exchanged by the two adjacent communities. Arrangements to facilitate an understanding of the rural-urban interdependent relationship could be executed efficiently and effectively by a pair of teachers—one from the rural area and the other from the urban setting—who teach children at the same grade level. The two teachers could complement each other by trading insights, objectives, methodological ideas, learning materials, and evaluative processes. At least three arrangements that the pair of teachers could consider suggest themselves: One might be to have their students study their respective communities and then to swap their findings. A second system would be for the urban children to direct their attention primarily to the rural community and vice versa and then for the two groups to corroborate, correct, and amplify each other's data and analyses. Still a third possibility could be for each class to look at both communities and then to exchange the results of their endeavors as a culminating activity.

In any event, the two groups of children could learn a great deal from each other about the two communities and the lines of mutual dependence existing between the divergent but unified environments. Many techniques could be developed by the pair of teachers. They might, for example, have each child draw the name of a pen pal in the class matched by grade level in the paired community. Pen pals could exchange facts and feelings, drawings, photographs, simple homemade maps, and so forth. Also, the teachers themselves could trade a number of relevant things. Each teacher might take color slides or photographs of *goods* going from his area to the neighboring community and vice versa and of *services* or *functions* performed by residents of his area upon which members of the adjacent community are dependent. The children in each of the two classes could tape-record interviews of local residents who are actively and continuously involved in the exchange of goods and services between the neighboring communities or might tape-record their own commentaries to accompany drawings, photographs, or slides sent to their friends in the other area. On an informal basis, parents of the children could be encouraged to take their youngsters on week-end drives in the paired community; to point out and explain to their children examples of interdependence; or to take photographs or slides (or help their youngsters take them) of representative illustrations of mutual dependence which could be used for class displays and discussions. On a more formal basis, the pair of teachers might arrange an exchange field trip. School busses transporting the urban and rural children could meet at a prearranged halfway point early one morning. The children might trade teachers for the day and travel around the contrasting area while their "teacher-for-a-day" would show and discuss with them aspects of urban-rural interdependence. Or, perhaps children from one of the communities could be bussed in for an afternoon to the paired school where drawings, photographs, maps, charts, graphs, tape recordings, individual and small group oral reports, etc., could be shared. Possibly, too, adults from each of the communities (a farmer, the manager of a farm co-operative or a wholesale produce outlet, a trucker, a feed salesman or farm equipment dealer, the superintendent of a meat packing plant or dairy, a retail grocer or restaurant owner, a farm building contractor, etc.) could be persuaded to serve as resource persons.

At the conclusion of the various activities devoted to helping the children discover the interdependence existing between the urban and rural communities, the pair of teachers involved might challenge their classes to develop as long a list as possible of goods and services exchanged from one area to the other. The two groups might even mimeograph a joint report pointing up contributions each of the communities makes to the way of life of the contrasting environment.

Our fourth basic generalization can also be illustrated through the use of various forms of literature. At the primary level, for instance, the teacher might read aloud to the class and invite a discussion of Jerrold Beim's *Two is a Team*.[24] The story deals with two youngsters, Ted and Paul, who quarrel about the correct way to build a roller coaster. Each decides to build his own, and, as each attempts to prove that his coaster is "better," they become involved in a series of unhappy incidents in which they knock down a woman's package, damage a child's doll, etc. Eventually they are asked to pay for the damage they have caused, and they finally decide to build one good wagon *together* and go to work as a team delivering groceries for a local store. Obviously the story illustrates a situation in which a problem was solved through co-operative efforts on a limited, face-to-face level.

With students in grades five through eight, the teacher could read *The Incredible Journey*[25] by Sheila Burnford, an excellent

---

[24] New York: Harcourt, Brace & World, Inc., 1945.
[25] Boston: Little, Brown & Co., 1960.

vehicle for helping youngsters look at the idea of interdependence in an allegorical fashion. This compelling story of an animal trio— a Siamese cat, an old bull terrier, and a young Labrador retriever— which travels 250 miles through the Canadian wilderness to find its owners makes it clear that, alone, any one of the animals would have perished on the trek, while together they were able to succeed. Each animal has his own unique talents and capacities, yet there are things each animal cannot do. It would not be difficult for the teacher to turn a discussion of the interdependent animals to a human societal situation.

The creative senior high school teacher might uncover numerous sources that could be read by students and discussed in class. The teacher might share brief passages with his students or compile a reading list so each class member could read something at his own developmental level and contribute his personal insights relevant to interdependence. After telling his class briefly the plot of *Of Mice and Men* by John Steinbeck—emphasizing especially the characteristics of George, the smaller more intelligent man, and Lennie, the powerful giant with the mind of a small child— the teacher might read this passage and encourage discussion of the interdependent relationship of brain and brawn which drew the two men together:

> "Well, I can go away," said Lennie. "I'll go right off in the hills an' find a cave if you don' want me."
> George shook himself again. "No," he said. "I want you to stay with me here."
> Lennie said craftily—"Tell me like you done before."
> "Tell you what?"
> " 'Bout the other guys an' about us."
> George said, "Guys like us got no fambly. They make a little stake an' then they blow it in. They ain't got nobody in the worl' that gives a hoot . . . about 'em—"
> *"But not us,"* Lennie cried happily. "Tell about us now."
> George was quiet for a moment. "But not us," he said.
> "Because—"
> "Because I got you an'—"
> "An' I got you. We got each other, that's what, that gives a hoot . . . about us," Lennie cried in triumph.[26]

There is a possibility, too, that a secondary teacher might like to have his students write their own essays around some theme of interdependence. Student essays might be stimulated by quotations such as the following:

---

[26] New York: Bantam Books, Inc., 1937; pp. 114–15. Copyright 1937 by John Steinbeck. Reprinted by permission of The Viking Press, Inc.

No man is an island, entire of itself; every man is a piece of the continent, a part of the main; if a clod be washed away by the sea, Europe is the less, as well as if a promontory were, as well as if a manor of thy friends or of thine own were; any man's death diminishes me, because I am involved in mankind; and therefore never send to know for whom the bell tolls; it tolls for thee.[27]

It is when we try to grapple with another man's intimate need that we perceive how incomprehensible, wavering, and misty are the beings that share with us the sight of the stars and the warmth of the sun.[28]

. . . [All] of us find that our own richest experiences in life come when we are sharing experience with certain other people or when we are acting with them to achieve some common goal. When other human beings are part of the environment, then the environment offers the possibility of greater inclusiveness, containing as it does then the value judgments, the purposes, and abstractions that can be shared and reacted to. Man's sense of active participation is, therefore, greatest when the environment through which participation is possible includes other human beings with purposes and capacities similar to his own.[29]

5. Every Group Is a Complex of Roles. Group Members Perform Given Roles and Have Some Understanding of the Expectations Associated with Those Roles. As a Member of Various Groups, a Person May Learn and Assume Different Roles During a Particular Period in His Life and at Various Stages in His Development and Maturation.

A role is a learned behavioral pattern assigned to and performed by a person as he interacts with others in a group. It encompasses an individual's expectations regarding others and the expectations directed toward him in a social milieu. A role includes privileges and disprivileges, rights and duties, and freedoms and responsibilities that cluster around a given position in a particular group. Every person learns to carry out one or more roles as he is exposed to a continuous series of situations involving human interaction. These roles can be stable or constantly shifting, compatible or incompatible.

27 John Donne, *Devotions* (London: William Pickering, 1850), p. 100.
28 Joseph Conrad, *Lord Jim* (London: John Grant, 1925), pp. 179–80.
29 Hadley Cantril, *The "Why" of Man's Experience* (New York: The Macmillan Co., 1950), p. 136.

An individual performs multiple roles at some stage in his development, and he also carries out various roles from time to time as he matures. He handles his roles with differing degrees of success and efficiency. In one role he feels confident and secure, and in another he is unsure and insecure. He experiences little conflict in this role and more conflict in that role.

No one finds it an easy task to learn to play a host of roles in a satisfying, sensible, consistent, integrative fashion. There are many demands and pressures to which an individual is subjected in a complex society. Of course, he often receives generous amounts of "help" from society in mastering roles, whether he requests it or not. The individual must learn roles in order to become a socialized participant in a society and a functioning member of a group.

One's understanding of a society is incomplete unless he has some insight into its roles and role expectations. This insight can be sharpened through an examination of the kinds and number of roles that exist in a particular society; the ways in which roles are taught, learned, and reinforced; the interrelationships and conflicts between and among roles; the attitude held with reference to given roles; the satisfactions derived from the performance of certain roles; and the alterations in roles resulting from changes in the individual and in the society. The more refined this insight is, the more accurately one can predict the behavior of a person or a group under carefully specified conditions. Being able to depend on others to behave in a given way because they occupy certain roles contributes to the stability of social interactions.

We believe that this sociological generalization dealing with societal roles—the final major idea we have pinpointed for illustrative purposes—could be utilized in many meaningful and interesting ways in our elementary and secondary schools. The examples offered below should trigger some purposeful, creative thinking on the part of classroom teachers.

There are at least four aspects of role as viewed from the perspective of a sociologist that seem to lend themselves to some study in our elementary and secondary schools. One dimension is the idea of role itself. A second is the understanding that an individual may learn and play different roles during certain stages of development and maturation throughout his lifetime. A third facet is the perception that a particular person may assume numerous roles at a given period in his life. And a fourth is the understanding that an individual may be confronted by conflicts as a result of a single role or a group of roles he portrays. Our illustrations of classroom methods will be clustered around these four facets of role in the order in which we have listed them.

The idea of role itself can be approached at various levels of complexity, of course. At the primary level, for example, the classroom teacher might unwrap this idea by asking class members to think of as many activities as possible that they have observed *people* (initially, the teacher should not use terms such as *adults* and *children,* or *men, women, boys,* and *girls*) engage in. Without any comment, the teacher would write all of the children's contributions on the chalkboard under the heading "Things People Do." The list might include items such as the following:

THINGS PEOPLE DO

eat	hammer
sleep	saw
cook	vacuum rugs
wash dishes	wax floors
wash clothes	walk dogs
change babies' diapers	paint house
mow lawns	sew
wash windows	put up screens
drive cars	teach
drive trucks	put in telephones
run trains	dig holes
steer ships	play "Jacks"
fly planes	play "King of the Mountain"
wash cars	fix cars
plant flowers	pump gas
iron clothes	dust
dump wastepaper baskets	cut down trees
pick up garbage	watch television
dig up weeds	set tables
laugh	sell things
cry	put out fires
sing	stop cars at cross walks
dance	run cement mixers
read	put letters in mail boxes

After a substantial representative list has been compiled, the second step in this rather informal "programmed discovery" approach is for the teacher to ask the class to consider *which* people (and now the teacher is ready to move into categories differentiated by age and sex) in their society *do* the things that have been written on the board. At this stage the teacher may decide to give the class some direction by pointing to activities such as "run trains" and "play 'Jacks,'" which have a more clearcut sex-age orientation, and by asking the class a leading question like, "Who would run a train —a *man* or a *woman*, a *boy* or a *girl?*" Or, the teacher may simply start at the beginning of the class list with the question, "Who does this?" and let the children fumble a moment until they see that some form of categorization would facilitate their discussion. At any rate, a columnized system might be developed which might appear like this:

WHO DOES WHAT?

Everyone   Adults   Men   Women   Children   Boys   Girls

Children should find it hard to fit some activities under the headings that have been established. A good exchange should take place on specific items. All exceptions the children can introduce should be welcomed by the teacher. For instance, the class may point out that women do most of the cooking and floor waxing in American homes but that men are often cooks in restaurants and janitors in large buildings; that girls usually wash dishes to help their mothers unless a family has all boys, in which case one or more of the boys perform this task; that some fathers help mothers by changing babies' diapers, but that other fathers help mothers by doing other things around the house, such as putting up screens; and so on. Of course, the placement of activities is not of prime importance, but this class procedure is essential for the emergence of the idea of role and its societal connotations.

The next step is for the teacher to probe with class members a question like, "*Why* do some people do things that others do not do?" (Why do adults drive cars instead of children; why do men usually run big cement mixers instead of women; why do women usually handle common household chores such as preparing meals, washing dishes and clothes, etc., instead of men; why do boys play "King of the Mountain" more often than girls; and why do boys commonly take care of the lawn while girls do the dusting.) The children will observe that some activities require more strength and hence tend to involve men; demand more experience, thus greater maturity, and are therefore carried out by adults; are shaped by unique conditions in homes—such as the absence of a mother or father—and elsewhere in society; and so on. They will perceive that other activities are just a matter of custom in our society and may have various exceptions. As soon as understandings like these seem to be clear to the children, a final question could be asked by the teacher: "How do people learn to do different things?" Responses should clarify the point that given behavior in a society is learned and will therefore tie in nicely with the *socialization process* treated earlier in this chapter. Children will be able to see in time, through procedures similar to those sketched here, that in our society girls are taught some things and boys others; that parents have responsibilities that adults without children do not have; that adults are expected to perform certain tasks not required of children, etc. While a group of understandings relevant to the idea of role are already present, the teacher may wish to give a *name* to what the class has been discussing and could say simply, "The things we are taught and expected to do are called *roles*. In our country there are *roles* for *adults* and *children*, *men* and *women*, *boys* and *girls*. All of us learn roles in order to get along in the places where we live."

From this point on, the teacher and the class could continue to share examples of roles performed by people on television and in the newspaper, by adults and children known to them, and by class members themselves. The children could be invited to mention interesting role exceptions, too, like women bus and taxi drivers, a man who prepares all the evening meals for his wife because he enjoys cooking, a girl who likes to do the yard work at her house, and so on.

The idea of role could be developed with students from the intermediate through the senior high school grades at differing degrees of sophistication through a writing assignment where each student would be asked to deal with a topic like "What I Want to Be" or "My Plans for the Future" or "What I Want to Do with My Life." After the themes have been turned in, the teacher could read certain passages aloud from them—with the permission of each student involved, of course, and *without identifying the writer's name*. Following the reading of a given excerpt, the class would be invited to respond to questions like the following (depending upon the substance and context of the material):

Do you think that the person who wrote what I just read is a boy or a girl? Why?

If the person *is* a boy (girl), will it be easier or harder for him (her) to become or do what he would like to? Why?

Would you guess that this person was raised in the city or the country? Why?

Do you think that many people would like to do what this person would like to do? Why? Are there a lot of opportunities in America to do this sort of thing? Why?

What might be some of the advantages of doing what this person would like to do? Can you think of any problems a person doing this for his life's work might have?

Such a line of questioning might reveal many student comments that could be directed toward a grasp of the idea of role. Students might point out that, while there may be exceptions, people still tend to think of a *man* as a doctor, a lawyer, a minister, a college professor, a mathematician, an airplane pilot, an army or police officer, a machinist, an assembly-line worker, etc., and a *woman* as a nurse, an elementary teacher, a secretary, a hair dresser, etc. The point here is not whether people's occupational preconceptions are *good* or *bad*, *right* or *wrong* (though a discussion at some other time could certainly deal with discrimination in various occupations), but that people do hold certain expectations about what men and women should do. Also, students could discover that one's experiential base (including an urban or rural background, a socio-economic orientation, a value system, the opportunity he has had to observe various roles portrayed, the roles he has been taught to assume, etc.) gives him certain perceptions, inclinations, and aspirations that can shape behavior today and tomorrow. At a concrete, meaningful level, the teacher can guide his students toward some understanding of what roles are, how they are transmitted and internalized, what their implications may be, and so on. The teacher can present a simplified sociological definition of *role* and assist students in illustrating and amplifying it.

With reference to the second aspect of role—the understanding that an individual may learn and play different roles during certain stages of development and maturation throughout his lifetime—the senior high school teacher could read aloud this familiar passage from Shakespeare's *As You Like It* to launch a discussion:

All the world's a stage,
And all the men and women merely players:
They have their exits and their entrances;
And one man in his time plays many parts,
His acts being seven ages. At first the infant,
Mewling and puking in the nurse's arms.
And then the whining school-boy, with his satchel
And shining morning face, creeping like snail
Unwillingly to school. And then the lover,
Sighing like furnace, with a woeful ballad
Made to his mistress' eyebrow. Then a soldier,
Full of strange oaths and bearded like the pard,
Jealous in honour, sudden and quick in quarrel,
Seeking the bubble reputation

Even in the cannon's mouth. And then the justice,
In fair round belly with good capon lined,
With eyes severe and beard of formal cut,
Full of wise saws and modern instances;
And so he plays his part. The sixth age shifts
Into the lean and slipper'd Pantaloon,
With spectacles on nose and pouch on side,
His youthful hose, well saved, a world too wide
For his shrunk shank; and his big manly voice,
Turning again toward childish treble, pipes
And whistles in his sound. Last scene of all,
That ends this strange eventful history,
Is second childishness and mere oblivion,
Sans teeth, sans eyes, sans taste, sans everything.

After the excerpt from Shakespeare has been discussed, clarified, and conceptually enlarged, students should find it easy to find contemporary examples. The teacher could then ask why these role shifts come about, whether every individual has the same pacing throughout the years as his neighbor, whether developments are identical from society to society and culture to culture, and so on.

The next passage could be used with both junior and senior high school students in a fashion similar to the quotation from *As You Like It*, for it also deals with the roles one man—this time a very real and great man—played during various periods in his life. In this moving excerpt from his autobiography *Up From Slavery*, Booker T. Washington describes the feelings he had upon receiving a letter from Harvard University inviting him to come to Cambridge to receive an honorary degree:

> This was a recognition that had never in the slightest manner entered into my mind, and it was hard for me to realize that I was to be honoured by a degree from the oldest and most renowned university in America. As I sat upon my veranda, with this letter in my hand, tears came into my eyes. My whole former life—my life as a slave on the plantation, my work in the coal-mine, the times when I was without food and clothing, when I made my bed under a sidewalk, my struggles for an education, the trying days at Tuskegee, days when I did not know where to turn for a dollar to continue the work there, the ostracism and sometimes oppression of my race,— all this passed before me and nearly overcame me.[30]

With children in the primary and intermediate grades, the teacher could handle this second facet of role by asking children to

---

[30] New York: Bantam Books, Inc., 1900; p. 209.

secure a set of photographs from a grandparent or an older neighbor which show the person from his childhood on through to his present age. The right collection of pictures could be really helpful in portraying simply, directly, and dramatically the roles that the individual has assumed. The photographs could be arranged in chronological order on a bulletin board or projected on an opaque projector. Pictures should be of obvious roles which the children could easily identify and discuss, such as the following:

(1) In mother's lap; 2 years old. (Son role.)
(2) Wearing Boy Scout uniform; 12 years old. (Boy Scout role.)
(3) In baseball uniform; 16 years old. (High school baseball player role.)
(4) Wearing graduation robe and mortarboard; 21 years old. (College student role.)
(5) Standing next to bride; 23 years old. (Husband role.)
(6) Holding baby; 25 years old. (Father role.)
(7) Sitting in office; 32 years old. (Businessman role.)
(8) Standing in front of church with minister; 46 years old. (Deacon role.)
(9) Holding baby; 52 years old. (Grandfather role.)

The third dimension of role, concerning multiple roles portrayed by an individual at a specific period in his life, could be approached at various grade levels through a simple but effective technique—a role diary. This procedure would be employed only after students had some feeling for the nature of role and role behavior. Each student would be asked to carry a small pad of paper with him for one week and to note each of the roles he plays during that short space of time. Students would be surprised at the rapid growth of their list if they are alert. Each class member might share his week-end enumeration of roles with the class, or all students could turn in their sheets and a committee could compile a master list. These are just a few of the items which might appear on such a list:

son	student
brother	choir member
grandson	YMCA member
nephew	neighbor
cousin	friend

The secondary school social studies teacher might initiate an interesting and meaningful discussion of the roles an individual can assume simultaneously through the use of material such as the following, which presents Lyndon B. Johnson's perception of his various roles when he was a member of the United States Senate:

> I am a free man, an American, a United States Senator, and a Democrat, in that order. I am a liberal, a conservative, a Texan, a taxpayer, a rancher, a businessman, a consumer, a parent, a voter, and not as young (50) as I used to be nor as old as I expect to be—and I am all of these things in no fixed order. . .[31]

Teachers and their pupils can explore the fourth facet of role —that concerned with difficulties which confront people when they are faced with conflicting role expectations—at all levels of instruction. Teachers may prefer only to give their classes an awareness of the idea of role conflict and its importance, or they may wish to help students uncover some nuances that are part of a deeper understanding of this sociological idea.

To open a general discussion of role conflict, the teacher could turn to countless factual and fictional accounts which focus on individuals who are subjected to differing expectations because of one or more roles they occupy. For example, the teacher could read aloud a passage like the following, which, incidentally, would be appropriate for use at the senior high school level. It is from the novel *Arrowsmith* by Sinclair Lewis, which is filled with illustrations of conflicting role expectations to which the doctor-researcher, Martin Arrowsmith, is subjected. The passage quoted here appears toward the close of the book. Arrowsmith—the husband of a wealthy woman, the father of a young son, and a prominent member of the staff of a scientific foundation—is thinking of rejecting all of the expectations being imposed upon him in order to engage in pure research in a wilderness area removed from societal distractions. His wife is speaking to him about his urge to get away from it all and says,

> "Look here, Mart. You feel so virtuous about wanting to go off and wear a flannel shirt and be peculiar and very, very pure. Suppose everybody argued that way. Suppose every father deserted his children whenever his nice little soul ached? Just what would become of the world? Suppose I were poor, and you left me, and I had to support John by taking in washing—"
>
> "It'd probably be fine for you but fierce on the washing! No! I beg your pardon. That was an obvious answer. But—I imagine it's just that argument that's kept almost everybody, all these centuries, from being anything but a machine for diges-

---

[31] "My Political Philosophy," *The Texas Quarterly*, I, No. 4 (Winter 1958), 17.

tion and propagation and obedience. The answer is that very few ever do, under any condition, willingly leave a soft bed for a shanty bunk in order to be pure, as you very properly call it, and those of us that are pioneers—Oh, this debate could go on forever! We could prove that I'm a hero or a fool or a deserter or anything you like, but the fact is I've suddenly seen I must go! I want my freedom to work, and I herewith quit whining about it and grab it. You've been generous to me. I'm grateful. But you've never been mine. Good-by."

"Darling, darling— We'll talk it over again in the morning, when you aren't so excited. . . . And an hour ago I was so proud of you!"

"All right. Good-night."

But before morning, taking two suit-cases and a bag of his roughest clothes, leaving for her a tender note which was the hardest thing he had ever written, kissing his son and muttering, "Come to me when you grow up, old man," he went to a cheap side-street hotel. As he stretched on the rickety iron bed, he grieved for their love. Before noon he had gone to the Institute, resigned, taken certain of his own apparatus and notes and books and materials, refused to answer a telephone call from Joyce, and caught a train for Vermont.

Cramped on the red-plush seat of the day-coach (he who of late had ridden in silken private cars), he grinned with the joy of no longer having to toil at dinner-parties.[32]

One nuance relevant to role conflict which teachers working with children and youth of various ages might pursue is the difference between *intra-role* and *inter-role* conflict (though these sociological terms as such probably would not be used except at the senior high school level). *Intra-role* conflict occurs when an individual experiences differing expectations because of a *single* role he occupies. *Inter-role* conflict takes place when a person is subjected to divergent expectations due to *two or more* roles he performs. The teacher could write his own problem situations to help his students discover these two basic forms of role conflict. Students could discuss some situations, role-play others, and write about still others, depending upon the nature of the situation and the age of the students. We have developed two such situations just to give the teacher a feeling for this approach. The first passage could be used with children in the primary and intermediate grades and deals with intra-role conflict. In the *one* role of mother, Mrs. Epstein is faced with the differing expectations of two children.

---

[32] New York: The New American Library of World Literature, Inc., 1924; pp. 425–26. (All publishing rights held by Harcourt, Brace & World, Inc.)

Mrs. Epstein lives in an apartment with her children, Kathy and Ralph. Mr. Epstein, a sergeant in the army, will not be home for almost a year. Kathy is in the first grade. Ralph is in the fourth grade. Ralph is a Cub Scout, and tonight he is going to receive his Lion badge. He has worked hard to earn this award. He is excited about this evening, because his mother will pin his cloth badge on his uniform in front of all the other Cubs and their families. When Kathy and Ralph get home from school, Mrs. Epstein discovers that Kathy has a fever. Kathy had been coughing for the last two days. Her eyes sting and look red. Mrs. Epstein calls the doctor. He says that Kathy probably has the measles and that she should be put to bed right away. Mrs. Epstein puts Kathy into bed, and Kathy says, "Don't leave me, Mommy, 'cause I don't feel very good." Mrs. Epstein tells Ralph what the doctor has said and says that Kathy may be a very sick girl. Ralph asks whether his mother will still be at the Cub Scout meeting. Mrs. Epstein wants to be with Ralph, but she also feels she should stay home and take care of Kathy.

This second situation could be used with junior and senior high school students and is concerned with inter-role conflict. Students should perceive quickly that Mr. Marshall is confronted with a real problem as a result of his various roles, which are easily identified. As a coach, a summer employee, a father, a husband, and a son, Mr. Marshall occupies a group of roles which are in conflict as described here.

Fred Marshall has been the basketball coach at Thomas Jefferson Senior High School in Sycamore, Indiana, for the past three years. He is just beginning his fourth season. His teams have lost most of their games since he has been coach. The former coach, who retired, had an outstanding record. Marshall's principal, Harold Long, has told him confidentially that the Sycamore School Board may look for another coach for next year if the team does not have a good season this year. One of the poorer players on the Jefferson basketball club is the son of a prosperous Sycamore building contractor, Alfred Spencer. Marshall has worked for Spencer the last two summers to earn extra money. And the contractor contributed $200 recently toward the purchase of new uniforms. Spencer has hinted several times that he would like to see his boy in the starting line-up. Further, Marshall's son Ted has turned out for the team this year and expects his father to give him an opportunity to play, even though this will be his first year of varsity basketball. Marshall's wife does not want their son to play basketball. She feels that the boy should devote more time to his studies so he will do well academically in college. She is worried, too, that her husband will be criticized by townspeople for displaying favoritism if he permits their son to play too much. Finally, the health of William Marshall, the coach's father, is failing and he has asked Fred to leave coaching after this season to return to his former home in another city and take over a small insurance business that his father has built up over the years.

CONCLUSION

In *The Two Cultures: A Second Look,* C. P. Snow rephrases the essence of his earlier lecture *The Two Cultures and the Scientific Revolution* in these words:

> . . . In our society (that is, advanced Western society) we have lost even the pretence of a common culture. Persons educated with the greatest intensity we know can no longer communicate with each other on the plane of their major intellectual concern. This is serious for our creative, intellectual and, above all our moral life.[33]

While *The Two Cultures and the Scientific Revolution* has been criticized for its tendency to overgeneralize and stereotype, it does identify a problem worthy of thorough consideration. This issue is the difficulty of establishing, maintaining, and enriching the exchange of thought, concerns, feelings, and projected visions of a better tomorrow among various groups. It would appear that some balance between general and special education and education in the humanities and the sciences should be maintained if we hope to facilitate the sharing of ideas and insights and to achieve some consensus among men of good will. Perhaps it is impossible for any individual today to exemplify the renaissance spirit found in such generous quantities in men like Leonardo da Vinci and Thomas Jefferson, but John Jones and William Smith must have some conversance with their physical, social, intellectual, aesthetic, and moral world and its cultural, ideological, scientific, and technological legacy.

---

[33] New York: The New American Library of World Literature, Inc., 1964, p. 59. (All publishing rights held by Cambridge University Press.)

With improved sociological offerings in our elementary and secondary schools, or materials which are embued with sociological insights, and with even better offerings in our colleges and universities, perhaps we will one day see more individuals who can think and operate comfortably and effectively in different fields. Hopefully, more and more fragments of knowledge can be combined into meaningful wholes. With time, possibly more people will typify the sensitive social perspective displayed by men like Albert Einstein, the physicist, in this passage which might have been written by a sociologist:

> When we survey our lives and endeavours we soon observe that almost the whole of our actions and desires are bound up with the existence of other human beings. We see that our whole nature resembles that of the social animals. We eat food that others have grown, wear clothes that others have made, live in houses that others have built. The greater part of our knowledge and beliefs has been communicated to us by other people through the medium of a language which others have created. Without language our mental capacities would be poor indeed, comparable to those of the higher animals; we have, therefore, to admit that we owe our principal advantage over the beasts to the fact of living in human society. The individual, if alone from birth, would remain primitive and beast-like in his thoughts and feelings to a degree that we can hardly conceive. The individual is what he is and has the significance that he has not so much in virtue of his individuality, but rather as a member of a great human society, which directs his material and spiritual existence from the cradle to the grave.[34]

---

[34] *The World as I See It*, trans. Alan Harris (New York: The Wisdom Library, 1949), p. 8.

Vocational Opportunities in Sociology

Sociologists do one or a combination of the following things: teach; do research; or deal directly with people in an administrative, counseling, therapeutic, or advisory capacity. Usually a sociologist teaching at the university level, engaged in independent research, or supervising a large number of people must have his doctorate. There are numerous jobs in the field, however, that require only a bachelor's or master's degree.

TEACHING

The field with the largest number of jobs in sociology is, of course, teaching. To teach at a university or to do independent research requires an advanced degree, usually a Ph.D. Some two-year terminal or junior colleges now teach sociology, and a few high schools have sociology courses. If these trends continue, there will be many more teaching jobs for sociologists holding only the B.A. or M.A. degrees. Nursing schools, medical schools, and departments of social work and education often require their students to have sociology courses. They hire people with B.A. degrees in sociology or with combination degrees, since this task requires competence in more than the field of sociology and does not require a person trained to do sociological research.

CRIMINOLOGY

There are numerous uses for sociology in the field of criminology. Parole officers are frequently trained in sociology. Policemen, policewomen, and prison guards are often given in-service training by sociologists on juvenile delinquents and adult criminals and why they behave the way they do. In large cities in both the North and South, the police are frequently taught something about the problems of minority groups and how to get along in dissatisfied segregated communities without provoking incidents. A state or a large city will often hire its own sociologist to do this training. Superintendents of prisons, reformatories, and jails and the officers of juvenile courts and youth commissions are usually trained in criminology.

SPECIALISTS IN THE FAMILY

Churches, general and mental hospitals, public or private welfare agencies, schools, city, state, and federal park systems, unions, and industry hire sociologists specializing in the family. Sociologists serve as marriage counselors, give advice on children's problems, give vocational and legal advice to family members, operate programs for retired people, and plan recreational programs for adolescents for these agencies and institutions.

INTERGROUP RELATIONS

Most of the people working in the growing field of intergroup relations are trained in sociology. The staffs of the Fair Employment and the Fair Housing Practices Commissions are sociologists. Most northern and western states and many cities have commissions of this kind. The United States Employment Office, many federal agencies, employer's associations and large industries, advertising councils, and national unions are hiring minority group experts at an ever increasing rate. The defense organizations of minorities like the National Association for the Advancement of Colored People (NAACP) or the Anti-Defamation League of B'nai B'rith (ADL) have some sociologists on their staffs. Many national and international church organizations, newly concerned about race relations, are beginning to hire experts in the field.

COMMUNITY RELATIONS

Experts in community relations are finding new openings. Any organization which has to deal with community disruptions, such as agencies providing new housing or engaging in urban renewal, usually hire sociologists to help people through difficult transition stages. A number of projects are being conducted in disorganized communities in large cities to build the morale of the community and to encourage participation in community life. It is too early to assess the effectiveness of these projects, but if they are successful they will be copied all over the United States. Their staffs are composed partly of sociologists. Rural sociologists have served for a long time as community consultants both to well-organized and to depressed rural communities, and they have been very much in demand by UNESCO, other international agencies, and the U.S. State Department to work in underdeveloped countries. These countries are, of course, mostly rural and exhibit the kinds of problems with which rural sociologists are familiar.

EXPERTS ON PUBLIC OPINION

Many workers in public opinion are trained in sociology. This is one of the fastest growing fields of employment in the United States. Anyone interested in knowing the attitudes of a large section of the American public at any particular time and about any particular subject hires a public opinion expert. This kind of knowledge is useful to large industries and business associations, national unions, politicians and political parties, advertising agencies, newspapers, TV and radio chains. Sometimes this information is sold by businesses which specialize in taking polls, like the Gallup Poll. Sometimes universities or foundations have polling organizations which provide information about attitudes to scholars and research scientists. Polling organizations of both kinds hire many sociologists.

INDUSTRIAL SOCIOLOGY

Business, industry, and labor often hire sociologists. Many personnel directors are sociologists. The industrial sector of the economy supports much social research, some of it directed to specific problems, but much of it of general interest. A large part of this is sociological research.

MEDICAL SOCIOLOGY

Doctors and psychiatrists have become increasingly aware of the relevance of sociological findings to therapy. Medical research and new therapy is very often conducted by teams which include a sociologist along with medical and psychiatric personnel. Hospital administrators have found sociologists very useful in devising ways of raising morale among staff and patients.

DEMOGRAPHERS AND ECOLOGISTS

Some city planners are trained in ecology and hired by planning commissions. Demographers make up most of the enormous staff of the Census Bureau. Insurance firms hire population experts to make up actuarial tables on which insurance rates are based. Telephone companies, power companies, schools, or any group interested in the size of future populations hire demographers. International agencies also use them frequently.

FREE LANCING

Some sociologists free lance and offer their specialized services to firms which cannot afford to hire a full-time sociologist, much as some certified public accountants do. One sociologist told an investment firm he could, on the basis of his sociological knowledge, predict those areas in which the firm should invest, and that he would be satisfied with a percentage of the profits. Among other things, he told them (in 1945) to buy stock in a firm that manufactured school desks, on the basis of his knowledge of the increase in the birth rate and the inevitable increase in school-age children. He and the firm made a killing. This sounds simple, but apparently no one else thought of it!

Professional Societies and Learned Journals

appendix two

The American professional society to which most sociologists belong is the *American Sociological Association* (ASA). Its purpose is to maintain communication among sociologists to exchange and further knowledge in the field; to set up requirements for admission to the profession and to establish codes of ethics; to organize the job market; to serve as a liaison with government, industry, labor, and other social organizations; to maintain contact with sociologists in other countries. The official organ of the ASA is *The American Sociological Review*, the main purpose of which is to publish research and to keep sociologists informed about matters of professional interest to them. There are also regional and a few state associations which publish journals.

One of the results of the growth of sociology is increased specialization and a rapid accumulation of knowledge, creating the problem of how communication is to be maintained both among the practitioners within a specialty and among those in different specialties. To handle these problems sociologists form specialized associations. Although they are concerned with only a limited portion of the field, they perform for *their* members the same services as the ASA does for all sociologists. The specialized associations also publish journals.

In addition to the specialized sociological journals and the publications of the regional associations, some universities publish sociological journals. The oldest and best known of these is the *American Journal of Sociology*, published at the University of Chicago. Listed on page 111 are the major sociological societies and the most important sociological journals.

ASSOCIATION OR UNIVERSITY	JOURNAL
American Sociological Association	*The American Sociological Review* and *Sociometry* and *Sociology of Education*
Ohio Valley Sociological Association	
Pacific Sociological Society	*The Pacific Sociological Review*
Eastern Sociological Society	
Southern Sociological Society	
Midwest Sociological Society	*Sociological Quarterly*
Southwest Sociological Society	*Southwestern Social Science Review*
District of Columbia Chapter of the ASA	
American Catholic Sociological Society	*American Catholic Sociological Review*
Rural Sociological Society	*Rural Sociology*
Society for the Study of Social Problems	*Social Problems*
University of Chicago	*The American Journal of Sociology*
Atlanta University	*Phylon*
University of North Carolina	*Social Forces*
University of Southern California	*Sociology and Social Research*
New School for Social Research	*Social Research*
Washington University (St. Louis)	*Trans-Action*
UNESCO	*International Sociological Bulletin*

---

* *Trans-Action* is a very readable journal and should be of particular interest to the layman.

A Selected List of Sociological References

The great increase of sociological knowledge has led to the establishment of *Sociological Abstracts,* a publication which abstracts and classifies most of the important research in sociology to provide a complete and accurate summary of what is being done in each field. In addition, there are a number of published summaries of research in various fields as well as books of readings which make available in convenient form research material first published in the learned journals. Some of the most useful of these are listed below. They can be found in any good-sized library.

GENERAL SOCIOLOGY

Index to the *American Sociological Review.* (Classifies by author and subject all articles and book reviews for the first 20 volumes.)

Borgatta, Edgar F., and Henry J. Meyer. *Sociological Theory: Present Day Sociology from the Past.* New York: Alfred A. Knopf, Inc., 1956.

Coser, Lewis A., and Bernard Rosenberg. *Sociological Theory: A Book of Readings.* New York: The Macmillan Co., 1957.

Gittler, Joseph B. *Review of Sociology: Analysis of a Decade.* New York: John Wiley & Sons, Inc., 1957.

Gurvitch, Georges, and Wilbert E. Moore (eds.). *Twentieth-Century Sociology.* New York: Philosophical Library, Inc., 1946.

Lipset, Seymour M., and Neil J. Smelser (eds.). *Sociology: The Progress of a Decade.* Englewood Cliffs, N.J.: Prentice-Hall, Inc., 1961.

Merton, Robert K., Leonard Broom, and Leonard S. Cottrell, Jr. (eds.). *Sociology Today: Problems and Prospects.* New York: Basic Books, Inc., Publishers, 1959.

Roucek, J. S. *Contemporary Sociology.* New York: Philosophical Library, Inc., 1958.

Schuler, Edgar A., *et al* (eds.). *Readings in Sociology.* 2nd ed. New York: Thomas Y. Crowell Co., 1960.

SOCIAL PSYCHOLOGY

Maccoby, Eleanor E., Theodore F. Newcomb, Eugene L. Hartley (eds.). *Readings in Social Psychology.* 3rd ed. New York: Holt, Rinehart & Winston, Inc., 1958.

Rose, Arnold M. (ed.). *Human Behavior and Social Processes: An Interactionist Approach.* Boston: Houghton Mifflin Co., 1962.

Stoodley, Bartlett H. (ed.). *Society and Self: A Reader in Social Psychology.* New York: Free Press of Glencoe, Inc., 1962.

SOCIAL STRUCTURE

Bendix, Reinhard, and Seymour Martin Lipset (eds.). *Class, Status and Power: A Reader in Social Stratification.* New York: Free Press of Glencoe, Inc., 1953.

Etzioni, Amitai (ed.). *Complex Organizations: A Sociological Reader.* New York: Holt, Rinehart & Winston, Inc., 1961.

Rose, Arnold M. (ed.). *The Institutions of Advanced Societies.* Minneapolis: University of Minnesota Press, 1958.

SOCIAL PROBLEMS

Lee, Elizabeth Briant, and Alfred McClung Lee (eds.). *Social Problems in America: A Source Book.* New York: Holt, Rinehart & Winston, Inc., 1955.

Merton, Robert K., and Robert A. Nisbet (eds.). *Contemporary Social Problems.* 2nd ed. New York: Harcourt, Brace & World, Inc., 1965.

SPECIAL SUBJECTS

Berelson, Bernard, and Morris Janowitz. *Reader in Public Opinion and Communication.* 2nd ed. New York: Free Press of Glencoe, Inc., 1953.

Brim, Orville G., Jr. *Sociology and the Field of Education.* New York: The Russell Sage Foundation, 1958.

Burgess, E.W., and Donald J. Bogue (eds.). *Contributions to Urban Sociology.* Chicago: The University of Chicago Press, 1964.

Clausen, John A. *Sociology and the Field of Mental Health.* New York: The Russell Sage Foundation, 1956.

Clift, Virgil A., *et al* (eds.). *Negro Education in America: Its Adequacy, Problems, and Needs.* New York: Sixteenth Yearbook of the John Dewey Society, 1962.

Janowitz, Morris. *Sociology and the Military Establishment.* New York: The Russell Sage Foundation, 1959.

Kirkpatrick, Clifford. *The Family: As Process and Institution.* 2nd ed. New Ronald Press Co., 1963.

Miller, Delbert, and William H. Form. *Industrial Sociology.* 2nd ed. New York: Huber, 1964.

Ohlin, Lloyd E. *Sociology and the Field of Corrections.* New York: The Russell Sage Foundation, 1956.

Rose, Arnold M., and Caroline B. Rose (eds.). *Minority Problems.* New York: Harper & Row, Publishers, 1965.

SOME OF THE LEADING GENERAL SOCIOLOGICAL TEXTS

Broom, Leonard, and Philip Selznick. *Sociology.* 3rd ed. New York: Harper & Row, Publishers, 1963.

Chinoy, Ely. *Sociology.* 2nd ed. Evanston, Illinois: Harper & Row, Publishers, 1958.

Rose, Arnold M. *Sociology.* 2nd ed. New York: Alfred A. Knopf, Inc., 1965.

Index